Making Friends
With
Black People

Making Friends With Black People

NICK ADAMS

Dafina
Books

KENSINGTON PUBLISHING CORP.
http://www.kensingtonbooks.com

DAFINA BOOKS are published by

Kensington Publishing Corp.
850 Third Avenue
New York, NY 10022

All Kensington titles, imprints and distributed lines are available at special quantity discounts for bulk purchases for sales promotion, premiums, fund-raising, educational or institutional use.

Special book excerpts or customized printings can also be created to fit specific needs. For details, write or phone the office of the Kensington Special Sales Manager: Kensington Publishing Corp., 850 Third Avenue, New York, NY 10022. Attn. Special Sales Department. Phone: 1-800-221-2647.

Dafina Books and the Dafina logo Reg. U.S. Pat. & TM Off.

ISBN 0-7582-1295-X

First Kensington Trade Paperback Printing: March 2006
10 9 8 7 6 5 4 3 2 1

Printed in the United States of America

This book is dedicated to the memory of my mother,
Jewell Henderson,
who taught me how to make friends with everyone.
I'm sorry for cursing so much.

Acknowledgments

To my beautiful wife, Tasha. Thanks for your support, input and laughs. And the sex.

To my agent, Claudia Menza. Without your foresight, none of this would have happened.

To my editor, Karen Thomas, and all the fine folks at Kensington Books. Words on a page do not a book make.

A portion of the author's proceeds for this book will be donated to the Lupus Foundation of America. For more information, visit *http://www.lupus.org/*.

Contents

Part I. Terminology

Part II. Interaction

Part III. Music and Culture

Contents

Part IV: Politics and Society

PART I

Terminology

Chapter 1

The N Word

I should make it clear that I am, of course, referring to the word *nigger*. Lest you think I would begin a book about race relations with a lengthy essay on Neanderthals or necrophilia. I figured that if I was going to write about race, I might as well start by tilting at the biggest windmill in sight. White readers, I should warn you right now that if reading this particular epithet makes you uncomfortable, you're going to be in for a rough ride for the next few pages. In order to get you used to seeing it, I thought I would go ahead and desensitize you a bit. Feel free to say it out loud. This is one of the very few times you will be allowed to do so.

Nigger nigger.

There. You should be pretty numb by now. Let's continue. I doubt that any single word in the history of my people has caused more concern than the word nigger. To fully understand the word, we must examine its history. It is, of course, derived from the Latin *niggerentis* meaning "he who is able to find the beat." According to historians, it was first used in its modern

3

incarnation in 1786. Although some scholars disagree on the exact time and place, there is a consensus over the circumstance. Hiram Wordsworth, a young schoolteacher, was visiting relatives in Maryland when he literally bumped into a free black man. Despite the fact that Mr. Wordsworth was clearly at fault, he lashed out. "Nigger! Watch where you are going." The black man, an elderly gentleman named Benjamin Banneker, was dumbfounded. Mr. Banneker, a legendary man of science and mathematics, was so affected by this event that when he was asked by George Washington to join the team of surveyors who were to lay out the plans for Washington, D.C., he insisted on a condition. That he be allowed to allocate an area of the city for people of color. Banneker wrote to Washington:

" . . . we have long been looked upon with an eye of contempt; and we have long been considered brutish rather than human, and scarcely capable of mental endowments. Not only do I believe that all Negro's should be made free, I submit that we should be allotted an area of land in every city within this union. These lands will preferably be located in southwardly or easterly areas of these cities, far away from any major body of water and out of view of any mountains. I believe this will inspire Negroes to act as a positive representative of these neighborhoods and live to their fullest extent."

That's right. Benjamin Banneker was not only the first nigger, he was the first to suggest that black people "rep their 'hoods to the fullest." Now, let's fast forward into the future by a few hundred million niggers. Unless, that is, you thought that all of that Benjamin Banneker stuff was serious. If that's the case, you need to close the book, turn your funny bone on, open the book and start again. I mean who would fall for something like that? A black man helping design our nation's capital? That's crazy talk. Next thing you know you'll be telling me that a black man invented the stop light and the gas mask too.

To me, the most interesting thing about the usage of the word nigger is that the outrage over who uses it seems to have shifted during my generation's lifetime. I'm thirty-one. My parents and grandparents are the ones who struggled for years to define themselves on their own terms. Accordingly, they came to reject the derogatory epithets that white America often hurled at them. The most popular, of course, was nigger. (Personally, I've always felt that *spear chucker* and *Alabama porch monkey* were more poetic, but they never quite caught on.) Once polite white society understood that they could no longer use that term—in public at least—older black Americans shifted their frustrations toward an unlikely group. Young black Americans.

The most popular culprits were the rappers and Def Jam stand-up comedians who used the word unabashedly in their routines and songs. Where the older generation refrained from using the word in mixed company, the younger generation had no problems using it on stage, on screen and within earshot of anyone who was listening. When this intraracial rift surfaced, my first thought was, "Where the hell do they think we got it from?" It's not like we learned the word while watching *The Electric Company* on television.

"Nuh"

"Igger"

"Nigger"

It's not like the See 'n' Say we played with as a child had a spot between the pig and the cow that explained how to use the word. "The homeboy says, 'Nigga!!!'"

It's not like we went off to kindergarten and heard our teacher say, "OK, class. Are you ready to sing our favorite song? Theeeee niggers on the court jump up and down, up and down, up and down. The niggers on the court jump up and down . . . and slam the ball through the hoop."

We didn't invent the word nigger. We learned the word from them. We heard it in the kitchen. We heard it in the living room. We heard it in the car. Of course we wanted to use it when we grew up. What did they expect us to do, treat the word like we did religion and just forget about it once we grew up and moved away from home? This is a disturbing trend when it comes to intergenerational—did I just make up a word?—relationships. Older generations tend to view history through rose-colored glasses. Instead of being honest about the way things were, they put themselves up on a pedestal while holding the activities and achievements of subsequent generations in low regard. It's just like Tom Brokaw running off at the mouth about "the greatest generation" that came of age during the depression, fought WWII, and "built modern America." Of course, he conveniently omits that whole institutionalized racism, sexism, McCarthyism thing. And let's not forget the Japanese-American internment camps, the Native Americans being taken away from home and sent to schools where they were beaten if they spoke their tribal language, the immigrants who were considered "feebleminded" because they were poor, dirty, and couldn't speak English. You have to be a special kind of jackass to call a group of people who wouldn't share a water fountain with another man because of the color of his skin "the greatest generation any society has ever produced." So, I guess I'm saying it. Tom Brokaw is a jackass. Similarly, you have to be pretty foolhardy to use a word as powerful as nigger in front of young children and then expect them not to wield it like a samurai sword once they've grown up.

Nigger has been used by blacks to refer to each other for decades. It's a greeting: "Hey, nigger. What's up?"

It's a term of endearment: "My nigger! Welcome home!"

It's an admonition: "Nigger, please. What the hell were you thinking?"

It's a useful, powerful, meaningful word that black people have been using for generations. You would be a fool to think that we are going to stop using it now. And why should we? Yes, it conjures up purely negative images for some people. Yes, there are people who will only ever use it in its historically pejorative context. So what? That's their problem. Just because something can be used to do harm doesn't mean that it doesn't have any positive value. I could probably kill a man with a banana if I set my mind to it. Does that mean that we should ban the growth, sale, and consumption of all bananas? And if so, what's our stance on plantains? Are we prepared for the economic impact that the ban would have on the countries for which bananas are the chief export? And what about the 26,000 people who would lose their jobs if the Chiquita company were forced to close its doors? And what the hell would old people put in their cornflakes? Maybe we would be better off if we just let people use their own discretion with bananas? As for nigger, I know what the word means when I say it. That's all that matters. When I think positive thoughts about my best friends of color, I often *think* the word nigger. How crazy is that? If I'm watching an NFL film special on ESPN about the Dallas Cowboys' Super Bowl season of 1993, I might think, "I hope that nigger Blu is watching this." If I'm reading an article about the difficulties of maintaining the canals in Venice I might think, "That nigger Rashid is in Italy right now." Of course I don't think nigger as in "he's a lazy, shiftless, good-for-nothing." I think nigger as in, "he's a solid guy" or "he's so much fun to hang out with" or "he's a funny dude." Wendell, Jamal, Mike, Boo, Mike & Tim, Little Steve, James . . . all these guys are my niggers. In fact, someone could be walking into a bookstore right now and saying to no one in particular, "I didn't know that nigger Nick wrote a book! Good for him."

Since an end to the use of the word is nowhere in sight, I suggest we have fun with it. I've found a great way to entertain myself and I'm going to pass it along to my black readers now. If you're ever in traffic and a white driver cuts you off, here's what you do. Lean out of your window; give him the finger and yell, "Watch where you're going, nigger!" His response will probably be something like this, "You watch where *you're* going, you fucking tar baby!" A split second later, he'll probably catch himself and begin apologizing profusely. "Oh my God! I didn't mean that! You tricked me!" By that time, you've already driven away, laughing hysterically. You crazy nigger. It may seem harsh, but I just love the fact that black folks have taken ownership of the most powerful slur in the history of the English language. We can actually use nigger and other epithets to make white people uncomfortable now. Say it in front of them and you can see white people wince. I'm seriously considering changing my name to Jigaboo Pickaninny just to watch the receptionist squirm the next time I go to the dentist's office. "Mr. Picka . . . umm . . . Jiga . . . umm. Yes, you. The black guy who's laughing so hard. The doctor will see you now."

Of course, white America's use of the word has gotten considerable press in recent years. Basically, the argument is this. If black people can use the word as a term of endearment, can't white people? No. No matter how close we become, don't ever use the word in our presence. It may not necessarily ruin the friendship, but we'll definitely have to kick your ass. It's a rule. I don't care how many black friends you have. I don't care if you have your hair in cornrows while wearing a Phat Farm T-shirt at an R. Kelly concert. Just don't do it. Special consideration may be taken for really cool Puerto Ricans. Also, an exception can be made in the case of repeating lines from music, television shows, and movies. However, said lines must be extremely sharp and relevant, and you must be extremely cool. Are we all clear on that? "But, Nick. I don't understand why I don't get to use the word."

Believe it or not, there are white people out there who actually debate this issue. It's not enough for these people to hang out with black folks socially; they feel like they must be accepted into our innermost circle for some reason. This isn't Skull & Bones. There's no secret password. Using the word doesn't give you any special insight into our culture or our struggle. It certainly doesn't endear you to us. Just be content with being a cool white person. You took our music, you took our clothes, you took our slang and you're importing players from Europe and China just to keep us from totally dominating the NBA. Can't we have anything to ourselves? Damn! Black people don't get to be president, and white people don't get to use the word nigger. Can we just call it even now?

And why would you want to use it anyway? Why would any white person ever want anyone to hear that word coming out of his or her mouth? Especially a black person. Don't they realize that the second they utter that term, everyone's concept of them as an individual is immediately going to change? I have about a dozen different cutesy nicknames for both of my cats, but in front of my male friends I only refer to them by their proper pet names, Grizz and Newman. I know if they ever hear me calling my cats Grizzy Bean or Newmster Poomster, they'll never take me seriously ever again.

Even more annoying than white people who question not being able to use the word, are white people who question whether or not black people should use it. I once had a white friend tell me, "I just think it's such a vile, disgusting word. I don't understand why anyone would want to use it. Even black people." I can't imagine anything more arrogant and presumptuous. There are plenty of things that white people do that we don't understand. We don't understand why you keep buying Kelly Clarkson's records, but no one is stopping you from going into Tower Records. We never watched *J.A.G.* or *Walker, Texas Ranger*, but faithful white viewers kept those shows on the air for years without any complaint from black America. We're not stopping you from eating fruitcake. You don't have to understand why we want to use the word. It doesn't belong to you anymore. It's ours. We earned it. But I forgot that good, liberal, white people always know what is best for black folks. Or at least they always think that they do. It's because of this attitude that we've been lucky enough to experience some of the high points of our culture. Integration. Allow us to spend our money in white grocery stores, restaurants, and shops, but don't spend any of your money in black grocery stores, restaurants, and shops. And we wonder why there aren't as many black businesses any more. Thanks a lot. Bussing. Force children to wake up extra early and take long bus rides to attend schools far away from their neighborhoods with kids that they don't know anything about. Great idea. Vanilla Ice. "If they like to watch other black guys rhyming, dancing, and wearing silly clothes, they're gonna love watching a white guy do it!" Genius. I wish liberals would do us a favor and stop helping us.

Amazingly enough, the controversy surrounding the word nigger seems to have transitive properties as well. In 1999, the cultural baggage that is associated with nigger moved up one entry in the dictionary and attached itself to a completely different word. David Howard, head of the Office of the Public Advocate for the city of Washington, D.C., was having a conversation about funding with two of his employees. Howard, who is white, said that his office needed to be more "niggardly" with their funds. Before long, he was receiving phone calls from people who had heard that he had used a racial slur. Niggardly is a synonym for stingy and, according to *The Barnhart Dictionary of Etymology*, can be traced back to two Middle English words, nig and nigon. There is no mention of any racial context. That's how powerful the word nigger is. It creates controversy even when it *isn't* used. Can you imagine gay rights activists causing a stink because someone called someone else a maggot? I doubt that Asian-Americans would be upset because someone used the word "chunk." The fallout from the incident was so great that Howard felt the need to resign. Although he returned to his job a month later, his name was unnecessarily dragged through the mud because a lot of ignorant people decided to make a fuss. Apparently, our nation's capital has no problem re-electing public officials who are known cocaine abusers, but civil servants with impressive—if somewhat archaic—vocabularies are simply not tolerated. Maybe if he had used the word in a more D.C.-friendly way, the people would have let it slide.

"Hey Marion. Stop being so niggardly with that crack. Pass that pipe!"

Niggerlogue:

I have a confession to make. I'm probably not the best person to make an unbiased assessment on the usage of the word nigger. I have a history with the word that dates back to my infancy.

Born Jamile Amoa Adams, I have been known by my family and friends as Nick for my entire life. When I was born, I weighed in at over ten pounds. As a newborn, my head was so large that it wouldn't fit through the hole in the little T-shirt. They were forced to put a six-month-old sized T-shirt on me. (If you're wondering, I grew into it nicely. My hat size is a very average 7 1/8.) According to my mother, the first thing my father said when he saw me for the first time was, "That's a big nigger right there!" My father's affectionate term stuck. He kept referring to me as his big nigger.

"Have y'all seen my big nigger? He's got his momma's nose and his daddy's eyes."

This was 1973, and my mother wasn't too keen on the idea of her husband referring to his newborn son as a nigger in public. She implored him to come up with a better nickname. The only actual name he could think of bearing any similarity to the word nigger was Nick. The nickname stuck and the rest of my family followed suit. So, you see, I've been a nigger since birth.

Chapter 2

A Name I Call Myself

Not quite as sensational, but arguably more important historically, is the debate over which term is the socially accepted description of choice. First, we were Negro. Now, the term sounds extremely dated, but I've always liked the word. To me, it's incredibly regal and professorial. During the 1940s and 50s, it lent a certain scholarly tone to newspaper headlines like *Two Negroes Found Lynched. Police Question Why They Were Out So Late*. Negro was not without its drawbacks, however. Semantically, it was entirely too similar to nigger and it allowed white people to disrespect us even when using the proper terminology. I am of course referring to the popular "Nigrah" bastardization made popular by the likes of Bull Connors and George Wallace. It takes a special kind of idiot to take a word that sounds so fundamentally positive and twist it into a slur. That's how dedicated to being ignorant they were. Regardless of how stupid they sounded, part of me has to appreciate that. I can always respect excellence and commitment. Even in racism.

I'm not sure if it's because the word is so closely associated with the leaders of the time, but it seems as if Negro was the perfect term to describe these individuals. Adam Clayton Powell, Medgar Evers, Dr. Martin Luther King Jr., Malcolm X. All those men were most definitely Negroes. At least until they were arrested for protesting the disgusting treatment black people received at the time. Then, of course, they became niggers again. Negro was the suit and tie that the black community wore when we went out into the great big job interview of life. Stand up straight, look people in the eye, and don't let them mistreat you. You're a Negro. I think black Americans will always have fond memories of the word just because it was our initial foray into self-actualization. Negro represents the first time in our history that we dictated how we were going to be treated, represented, and labeled. "You, white man, must call me Negro. If you don't, polite society will shun you." Like all nascent attempts at maturity, we tend to remember it fondly. I think the first time I tried to shave myself with a disposable razor, I lost approximately one full pint of blood. But somehow, whenever I think back to it, it brings a smile to my face.

After Negro, came Afro-American. This one always confused me as a child. As a product of the 1970s, I assumed that it was somehow related to the Afro hairstyle. Although I didn't quite understand why an entire race would choose to so closely identify itself with a popular 'do, I accepted it. Understandably, I was even more confused in the 1980s when we did not switch to being referred to as Jheri curl-Americans, or High Top Fade-Americans. In retrospect, that would have lead to an extreme fragmentation of our society. Mullet-Americans, Feathered-Americans, Jewfro-Americans. Nope. Way too divisive.

Afro-American didn't have the organic sound of Negro, and it wasn't nearly as literally correct as its successor. It was the perfect term for the time though. Black people were in flux. We were in between. We were starting to be proud of our roots, and still demanding our rights as Americans. We needed a term that fit the times. Nothing says blackness circa the late 1960s and 1970s like Afro. Even now, saying the word Afro makes me want to put on a dashiki and hang up an oil painting of a beautiful black sister lounging around with a panther, light some incense, fire up a joint, turn over the Parliament LP, and groove. Dig? Solid.

We seem to have settled on African-American, and at first glance it certainly does seem logical. We are Americans who are decedents of Africa. Makes sense, right? Yes, but this term poses all kinds of problems.

First, once you get into hyphenating based on continent of origin, the obvious question is, "Do you have to do that for everyone?" Asian-American, European-American, South American-American . . . where does it stop? Not to mention what happens when hyphenates marry other hyphenates and have baby hyphenates. When they apply for college, my as yet unborn children might have to suffer through form after form listing themselves as Native-American/African-American-American.

Also, even though my ancestors were originally from Africa—for that matter, who's weren't?—I'm about as African as Mary Kate and Ashley Olsen. It seems disrespectful to African culture to refer to myself in that vein. I wear Nikes, I watch *South Park*, I eat fast food . . . I'm extremely American. It just seems totally arbitrary to label myself based on where my great-great-great-great-great grandmother or grandfather was stolen from. Besides, I could think of several other hyphenates that would be more appropriate. Dallas Cowboy-American, TiVo-American, Internet porn-American. Those all go a lot further in describing what kind of person I am than African-American. Don't get me wrong. If I had lived during Marcus Garvey's time, I would have been the first person on board the Black Star Line. Good idea, Marcus. Let's cut all ties with this racist cesspool of a country and start fresh on our own. (Although, given the way things turned out in Liberia, maybe that wouldn't have been such a good idea.) I look forward to the day when I can set foot on the continent. I realize that, ultimately, I am a son of Africa. But I was born and raised in Eden, North Carolina. I don't trace my lineage back to the Masai, Wolof, or Yoruba tribes. I trace it back through various Adams, Jumpers, Moreheads, and Meadows from all over the southern United States. I'm American, damn it. As corny and trite as that may seem, isn't that what my people fought so long and hard for? So that I could stand next to a lily-white Republican from Connecticut and feel just as American as him? At least until the cops come.

The last, and most obvious, problem with African-American is that it takes too damned long to say. Say it out loud. African-American. Seven syllables. It's quite a mouthful. And a clumsy one at that. It's not a lyrical mouthful that rolls off the tongue like *lugubrious* or *verisimilitude*. (Consult dictionaries . . . now. Don't sweat it. I didn't know what they meant either.) Whenever my wife and I go to Seattle to visit her family, I look forward to the stimulating conversations that I know we will have with my in-laws. They are smart, well-educated people who are always abreast of the political, social, and cultural issues of the day. They watch tons of movies and read tons of books. Both her parents are Native-Americans, so they take great pains to be sensitive when they are talking about other cultures. I remember my mother-in-law talking about a conversation that she had had with a coworker.

"I was talking with my friend James, who's an African-

American. He was saying that in the African-American community . . ." I felt like screaming, "What did that nigger say already?"

Which brings me to my personal favorite: Black. It makes more sense than the others in every way. Phonetically, it's no contest. One syllable versus multi-syllabic hyphenates. Black wins hands down. Although initially it doesn't conjure the lofty bourgeois imagery of the other terms, it depicts a more realistic portrayal of who we really are. Indeed, who we have become. And I don't mean that in a negative way. (I also don't mean that in a literal way. I have met some extremely dark people in my life, but I think very dark brown is the closest a human being can come to actually being black.) When my family put on our Sunday best and sat through a two-hour, fire-and-brimstone, Baptist church service . . . we were African-American. When we came home and changed into jeans for Sunday dinner . . . we were black. When I go into an office for a job interview . . . I'm African-American. Once I get the job . . . I'm black. Black is who we are and what we call ourselves when we aren't concerned with what white people think. It isn't lesser than. It isn't greater than. It just is. It's more casual, more understated, and much more honest.

The word is also vastly more organic than the alternatives. Over the years, while the cultural and political elite of black society were busy deciding what we should be called, we simply started referring to ourselves as black. It does not allow us to hang on to some old, bullshit ideal of what we are supposed to be. Or how we're supposed to look or act or think or dress or what kind of music we're supposed to listen to. Black says, "This is us. The best of us, the worst of us. Take it or leave it."

We were shown the way by different social, political, and cultural pioneers. Miles Davis, John Coltrane, James Brown, Malcolm X, Shirley Chisolm, Tom Bradley, Jackie Robinson, Jim Brown, Bill Russell, Ralph Ellison, Toni Morrison, Langston Hughes, Dr. Ronald McNair, Dr. Mae C. Jemison, Cornel West, Randall Robinson, Sidney Poitier, Ozzie Davis, Ruby Dee, Dick Gregory, Bill Cosby. These are all black people. Hear that? That's the sound of white readers running off to the Internet to do some serious research.

Being African-American means that you have to live up to a certain standard at all times. I like being black if for no other reason than that it's only one step removed from being a nigger. That way, if I act a fool at a concert or decide to hang out all night smoking weed and drinking malt liquor with Big E., I won't be ashamed or feel the need to apologize. Here's a little secret that black people don't want white America to know. There's a little nigger in all of us. *All* of us. Dr. King? Rumored to have been quite the ladies' man. Jesse Jackson? Fathered an illegitimate child. Al Sharpton? The hair. Enough said.

PART II

Interaction

Chapter 3

To Ebonics and Beyond!!!

I f we're going to learn to live together, obviously we have to spend time together. Quick. White readers, when was the last time you had a black person in your house? Oprah doesn't count. I don't mean Oprah isn't black, but she's not physically in your house. The cable guy and the UPS man don't count either. I mean an actual acquaintance of color that you invited into your home? Sad, huh? I'm not letting my black readers off the hook. I think during my entire childhood, the only white people who ever got near our house were Jehovah's Witnesses. With my mother and grandmother both being proud members of Mt. Sinai Baptist Church, I don't have to tell you that those Jehovah's Witnesses didn't get any closer than our front porch. Once, they actually had the nerve to ring our doorbell on Christmas morning. Luckily for everyone involved, those Jehovah's Witnesses were extremely fleet of foot. I can't imagine how much therapy it would have taken to deal with the memory of watching my mother beat a man to death with my brand-new Etch-A-Sketch.

If white people are going to spend quality social time with black people, obviously they'll have to learn how to talk to us.

Yes, I said learn. The sad fact is, most white people don't have a clue. I'm now going to outline the fundamentals for my white readers.

Slang. It's an extremely important part of conversing with any group. Black people have a wide array of colorful terms that come in and go out of style and can be used in a myriad of different ways. White people, it will be extremely tempting to try and incorporate these terms into your everyday language. Don't. If you are using a particular slang term, then it's probably out of date. When you guys start using our words, that's when we know it's time for us to stop using them. There's an e-mail list that we all subscribe to and every time a white, middle-aged, math teacher calls one of his students "dog," black people all over the country are immediately notified. Think about it. When was the last time you heard a black person actually refer to something as "the bomb"? It's been a while, hasn't it? That's because we don't use that one anymore. Thanks to white people, the use of that particular slang term is actually a misdemeanor in some states. Do us a favor. Stick to good old-fashioned Queen's English. Especially when it comes to the newer terms. Most black people over the age of twenty-five don't even bother with these anyway. They're strictly reserved for teenagers and those who don't have to hold down a nine-to-five job within earshot of white people. Hollering about how "crunk" that new Lil' Jon video is while you're in the copy room will not get you any closer to the promotion and the corner office. Also, you can't just learn the word. It's not that simple. You have to keep abreast of any updates or changes to its syntax or usage. What started out as "off the hook" became "off the heezy," which then became "off the heezy for sheezy," which begat "off the heezy for sheezy my neezy." Honestly, don't you have some-

22

thing better to do than keep track of the etymology of "heezy"? Not to mention the "chain" or the "Richter" or any of the other things that it's possible for something that is most excellent to be off of. I warn my white readers away from these words specifically because they've proven difficult to navigate even for a seasoned veteran of Negro vernacular like myself.

"Hey Nick, what did you think of that new Sam Jackson movie?"

"I thought it was pretty thumpity-thump thump."

"What?"

"Thumpity-thump thump?"

"Nigger, I have no idea what you're talking about."

"Man, I heard that shit on BET last night. I thought I'd give it a try. Screw it. That movie was dope!"

Now I stick to what I know. I restrict myself to vintage slang like "dope," "fresh," and "chillin." The classics never die.

Not that it isn't possible for white people to grasp the intricacies of these words, but most people aren't willing to put in the time that it requires to fully master the language. It's just like the difference between the Spanish you learn in high school and the Spanish that is spoken on the streets of Mexico City. You may have gotten an A in Mrs. Pryor's class, but you would probably get laughed out of any of the bars in the Polanco district. In order to become truly conversational with slang, you would have to spend hours and hours hanging out with black people and I've already documented that most white people just aren't willing to do that. That's why it's safest to just avoid slang all together.

The same hurdles present themselves when it comes to shaking hands with us. The "soul shake" or "dap" has been around for decades. New techniques are incorporated into the maneuver and classics are often resurrected for younger generations. When attempted by an overzealous white novice, the consequences can be embarrassing for both parties. Here's what happens. Anthony Blackdude is introduced to Whitey McBread. Anthony, who is a corporate attorney, extends his hand to give Mr. McBread a good firm handshake. Whitey, attempting to "connect" with Mr. Blackdude, tries to give him a nice soul shake the way he's seen the black guys do it before and after the pickup basketball games at the YMCA. He's dreamed of this moment. He's visualized it in his mind a thousand times. This is the opportunity of a lifetime and he's decided to seize it. The combination of Blackdude's firm, locked hand positioning and McBread's relaxed wrist combine to form a sloppy exercise that's impossible to correct without starting over completely. These two men, who may share a taste in football teams, movies and video games, have lost any chance that they may have had to strike up an immediate friendship. Whitey thinks that Anthony is a stuffed shirt, and Anthony thinks that Whitey is a limp-wristed sissy. Sad. If you must attempt the soul shake, your best bet is to go for the classic "grip, slide, grip, release" which is detailed here. First, come in strong, with your right forearm parallel to the ground and your open palm perpendicular to the ground. (See Fig. A.) Imagine that you are going in for a horizontal, medium-five. Don't aim for palm-to-palm contact though. You want your hands to hit at the heels of the respective palms so that your thumbs can interlock. Now, clamp your hand closed around his hand. Your hands should now resemble two people who are about to begin an arm wrestling match. (See Fig. B.) Now, open your hand again and slide it back toward you. Your palms should be brushing against one another's. Continue pulling backward until your fingertips are resting against his second knuckle. At this point, you will bend your fingers at your second knuckle, while he does the same. Your hands should now be clenched together as if you're beginning to thumb wrestle. (See Fig. C.) Congratulations! You have now given someone "dap." To learn more advanced techniques such as "the pound," the "dap with a snap," and others, buy a copy of my book, *The Complete Idiot's Guide to the Soul Shake*.

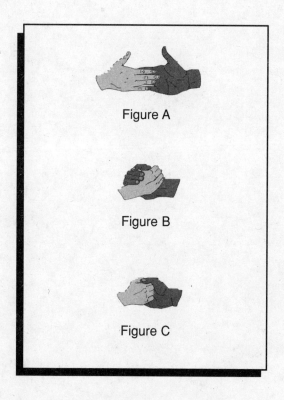

Figure A

Figure B

Figure C

Chapter 4

Ask Me No Questions

N ow that you've been taught our basic greeting, and been given some general advice for speaking to black people, it's time to get specific. Most conversations begin with a casual icebreaker. To the untrained white person, what seems like a harmless conversation starter can often be a recipe for disaster. There are quite a few potential land mines that you should try to avoid at all costs.

Don't try to start a conversation with a black person by using a topic that you assume we know a lot about. It may seem innocent enough to you, but somehow, it sounds different to us. If you were to try to find a common musical bond to share with a black person by asking, "So, that new Nelly album is great, right?" it would get filtered through 400 years of slavery, rape, and murder and come out sounding like this, "So, watermelon is great, right?" It's not your fault. Something gets lost in translation. Also, if it turns out that I'm not a particularly big fan of Nelly, it's just going to confuse you. "Doesn't he like hip-hop?" It would probably never cross your mind that one could be a fan of the genre without enjoying every group or artist within the genre. Personally, I love refuting this particular bias by having an extensive knowledge of seemingly ultra-white topics. Talk about fun. Nothing beats having a discussion about music at a party and being able to out-Steely Dan the white guy.

White guy: "I like their earlier stuff much better."

Me: "Yeah, but they didn't really come into their own until they stopped trying to find a core group of other musicians to depend on and just billed themselves as a duo. You can hear the difference all over *The Royal Scam* and, of course, the subsequent classic, *Aja*.

White guy: "Yeah. I guess you're right. So have you heard that new Nelly album?"

Don't ask us questions that start with, "How do black people do . . ." or "Why do black people do . . ." This is where being a nice guy can really hurt me. Instead of asking the less approachable black people that they come into contact with on a regular basis, most white people save all of their curiosity and wait until they meet someone seemingly less militant—that would be me—and hit them with a barrage of questions. Let me say this once and for all, white people. I am not the registrar of information for my entire fucking race. I have been shaving my head almost every day for the last ten years. How in the hell should I know how Marcus from accounting maintains his dreadlocks? Although, if you are an attractive white woman asking these types of questions of a single black man, you will probably get a much warmer reception. Every black man I know would be more willing to explain to Jessica Simpson, in detail, the intricacies of black hair care.

Me: "You see, Jessica, when white people get a perm . . . it curls their hair. When black people get a perm, it straightens their hair."

Jessica: "Nuh uh!"

Don't quiz us on our own culture, music or politics. Trust me; we know more about it than you do. So you just read *The Autobiography of Malcolm X* . . . big deal. There is nothing more annoying than facing some white person at the water cooler who's recently stumbled upon a juicy bit of ghetto trivia and can't wait to play a few rounds of everyone's favorite game show, "Stump the Black Guy."

"Hey Nick, do you know who played Thelma's husband on *Good Times?*"

"Ben Powers. Can we talk about football now?"

"Sure, did you know that when Jim Brown played football at Syracuse . . ."

"Yeah, he was on the lacrosse team too. He's in the Lacrosse Hall of Fame. Listen, I got some phone calls to return. I'll see you later."

Whenever white people get into this mode, I always feel like I'm Nipsey Russell on some bastardized version of the *$10,000 Pyramid.*

"Voting rights. Apostrophe 's.' Banks."

"Things that Black people don't use."

"Yes!"

No matter how tan you get on vacation, you aren't "almost as dark as me." Save the forearm comparisons. Besides, who are we kidding? Even if you did wake up one morning a few shades lighter than Wesley Snipes, you'd be too busy committing suicide to even make it in to work that day. White people want to be *darker*. They don't want to be *dark*. There's a difference. Dark gets pulled over by the cops three or four times before the 30-day tags on his Volkswagen Passat have expired. Dark saves his money and has good credit just so he'll be able to get a home loan . . . and then can't get a home loan. Dark is proud to be able to buy his wife something really nice for her birthday, only to be followed around the department store by a white security guard. Dark gets pulled out of the line just before boarding his flight to be part of a "random" passenger search. You guys should just stay pale and enjoy it. If it's good enough for Nicole Kidman—seriously, can we get her a blood transfusion already?—it should be good enough for you. (Nicole. If by any chance you are reading this, that last line was purely in jest. I actually think you are an extremely attractive woman. Although I am married, I would be open to the idea of having a friendly, platonic but *extremely* flirtatious lunch with you.)

Black men with dreadlocks do not automatically have in their possession or know where you can get marijuana. It's possible that they just like the hairstyle. Besides, even if he does know where you can get your hands on some of the good herb, I doubt he's going to share that information with a complete stranger. You'd be better off wearing a trucker hat with the word "Narc" written on it. Here's a tip. A white man with dreadlocks is much more likely to have embraced the entire lifestyle, including the drug that is associated with it. A black man with dreadlocks can put on a suit and be taken seriously in a place of business. You would let a black man with dreadlocks do your taxes. You would let a black man with dreadlocks teach you a class on screenwriting. If a white guy with dreadlocks fixes your ice-blended at Starbucks, you've got your eye on him the entire time.

"Fucking hippie."

If you find yourself starting a sentence, "No offense, but . . ." stop. Chances are we're going to be offended. Either you should be 100 percent certain that what you are about to say will not be deemed offensive, or you should have the common sense to not say it. I know I'm the friendly black guy that you think you can bounce your edgy ideas off of, but just because I don't wear my black rage on my sleeve doesn't mean it's not there. Lucky for you, most black people manage to keep their tempers in check. If that weren't the case, the office buildings of America would be littered with the corpses of white people who thought, "Now is the time. I'm finally going to tell LaShonda what I think about affirmative action."

Don't tell us that you "don't see color." Aside from being trite and patronizing, it's just plain stupid. The fact that you can see me and treat me as an individual regardless of my race is great and all, but does that mean that your rods and cones have ceased to function and you can no longer discern that my skin is darker than yours? Let's leave the term color-blind for dogs and the 8% of the population who do actually suffer from the affliction. If you are color-blind, you get a pass because you've got bigger problems to worry about. Like not being able to tell that the marble rye bread you are about to eat is green in some spots. But everyone else needs to knock that shit off.

This one is for the other minorities who might be reading this book. Don't try to compare stereotypes with us. You can't win.

Ours are much worse. This goes double for Jews and Asians. Try lazy, horny, ignorant, and violent on for size. I'll take being considered greedy and good at math over those any day of the week. And while we're on this subject . . . good at math? Is that the best stereotype that we can come up with for Asian people? There are over a billion Chinese people alone. You would think that with the sheer number of Asians that exist on the planet, we would have come up with something better than good at math. If there are any racists reading this book, go ahead and get started on that.

The only group that can possibly complain to black people are Native Americans, but even their stereotypes are getting better. They went from "they're all drunks" to "they're all rich from casinos." It warms my heart to see people's stereotypes progress. Now, if all of the Native peoples who are living well below the poverty line would just get off their asses and go claim the huge casino checks that are being held for them. What are they waiting for?

We all know that these stereotypes aren't true. Black people are supposed to be lazy. Lazy? Didn't people see the riots in South Central Los Angeles back in 1992? We destroyed over a thousand buildings. That's hard work. We worked all day and well into the night. Let's see a white person try to burn down an entire liquor store with a crack pipe and some old newspaper. That's real Boy Scout stuff. Black people called in sick to their jobs . . . and then went out looting! Now that's dedication.

And it's just as foolish to call Jewish people greedy. I have found Jews to be incredibly giving people. They give us credit cards. They give us bank loans. They give us roles in their motion pictures and television shows. When will people ever learn? But back to that Asian stereotype. Asians *are* smarter. It's a fact.

Making Friends With Black People

Unless you can name a single feat that any other ethnic group has achieved that's more impressive than eating an entire seven-course meal using only two thin wooden sticks as utensils? That's what I thought. My wife has a friend who's half Asian and half Jewish. I can't help but wonder how that combination played out growing up. She tells her parents that she wants to go to summer camp and they freak out.

"No! Nothing with camp in it. No summer camp, no concentration camp, no internment camp. None of that stuff. You can go to the YMCA day camp, but I want you in this house by 6 P.M. every night!"

And now that I think of it, Jews are greedy. Think about it. They get to take advantage of Christian holidays like Easter and Christmas, but then they also get the Jewish holidays, too. Well, from now on I'm not letting those greedy bastards get over on me any more. I can't even pronounce their holidays, but I'm taking them off.

"Yeah, I won't be coming in tomorrow. It's Ross Shoshonna."

"Who?"

"It's umm . . . Tom Kemper?

I don't look anything like him. No, I don't. I don't look anything like Shawn, Keith, Charles, Leon, Randy, Ed or any of the other black people you know. I think I can safely speak for every other black person on the face of the planet when I say, "Look at my fucking face!" I know there is another bald black guy that works over in the Swinden office, but also having dark skin and also shaving his head isn't enough to make him the identical twin of the guy in the cubicle next to yours. If black people can devote the time and energy required to figure out the difference between Owen and Luke Wilson, I think you guys can do it for the three or four black people that you interact with on a daily basis. It may sound like a small thing, but what is more dehumanizing than this? Basically, what you're saying is the following: "Even though I see you all the time, I don't feel that it's necessary to make an effort to commit your face and name to memory. Nigger." OK, you may not be thinking that last part, but you know what I mean.

Along the same lines of this phenomenon, I've noticed that a lot of white people don't seem to recognize me out of context. The same people that can chat with me in the laundry room of our apartment complex or on the sidelines at the basketball courts are totally dumbfounded when I approach them in the grocery store to say hello. The second that I'm taken out of their frame of reference, it's like I cease to exist. Now I know what it feels like to be Nick Lachey.

Yes. We love soul food. We grew up eating it. Black-eyed peas, cornbread, collard greens . . . all of that stuff is great. We've moved on. We eat sushi now. I don't want to go to lunch with you to Sylvia's, Aunt Kizzy's Back Porch, or Aunt Jemima's Coon Emporium or whatever soul-food restaurant you read about in the weekend section of the local newspaper just so you won't feel as uncomfortable as you would if you went by yourself or with another white person. You want to bond with us? Let's bond over some unagi. And that goes double for any restaurant that bills itself as cooking "healthy soul food." That doesn't exist. If it wasn't fried in lard, or simmered with pork until all the nutrients are gone, then it isn't soul food. Don't get me wrong; I have nothing against soul food. It's slave food that I can't eat. Slave food is chitlins, pig's feet, and all that other shit that our people ate out of pure necessity back in the day. "Hey!

34

Massa say we's only get that one pig to las' all of us fo' de whole week. Don you throw that snout away! And keep dem feets too!"

There's no need to dump a bunch of hot sauce over something that should be considered inedible and call it an ethnic delicacy. Chitlins are the perfect example. (I type it in the colloquial form because I can't bring myself to type out chitterlings. See? That just looks silly.) Like most "delicacies," chitlins are quite disgusting when you get down to it. What are they, you ask? The boiled large intestines of a pig. On top of the repulsive nature of the food itself, chitlins stink up the entire house when you cook them. It's a rancid, acrid, aggressive smell that gets into every nook and cranny of your home. It's the kind of odor that makes you self-conscious for days after the fact. A week later as you get dressed for school or work, you'll be saying, "I think I *still* smell like chitlins!" It's so foul; I don't even have the necessary word power to describe it to you. It smells like . . . it smells like . . . it smells like someone is boiling pig intestines in your kitchen. It is mind-boggling that white people are worried about having chemicals and additives in their food when some black people don't even have food in their food. Can we get some damn integration in the meat department?

Hate groups like the Ku Klux Klan and the Aryan Brotherhood should build their entire platform around chitlins. It's the most effective rebuttal that the racist has in any argument. How smart can a group of people be if they still eat pig guts, right?

"But Mr. Grand Wizard, African-Americans are doctors, lawyers and politicians. They've helped cure diseases, discover continents, and have traveled into outer space. Surely you don't really believe them to be inferior do you?"

"They still eat chitlins don't they?"

"Touché, Grand Wizard. Touché."

Ethnic "Delicacies"

Lest you think that black folks are the only ones with strong stomachs. Here are some other examples of ethnic delicacies. The lesson to be learned here? We are **all** disgusting.

Chitlins (US) The aforementioned offal as food. I don't know about you, but when I get hungry, I think intestine.

Menudo (Mexico) No. I'm not talking about the Puerto Rican boy band. (Although I'm sure those guys are delicious.) I'm referring to the Mexican dish of the same name. If you ask someone to tell you what menudo is, they'll tell you that it's a stew made with tripe. What they won't tell you is exactly what tripe is. I love it when people try to trick you by giving things a more palatable name.

Scenario #1:
"Would you like to try a traditional Mexican dish called menudo?"
"Sure, that sounds great."
Scenario #2:
"Would you like to eat the stomach lining of a cow?"
"Gross. I think I'm just gonna stop by Subway instead."

Yeah, that's what tripe is. The stomach lining of a cow. The second definition of the word tripe tells you all you need to know: Something of no value; rubbish.

Haggis (Scotland) OK, white people. You can stop looking down your noses at us now. Straight from the Scottish highland comes haggis, a sausage that's made using a sheep's heart, liver and lungs and boiled in the animal's stomach for several hours. And just to give it that special touch, sometimes they throw in the intestines. Although it's widely available in Scotland, you might have a hard time getting your hands on the real deal here in the US. Why? Seems as if our laws forbid the sale of any animal's lungs for human consumption. Let me get this straight. You can suck on super-addictive, lung-damaging, cancer-causing cigarettes all day long if you want. But you can't eat sheep lungs? Yeah. That makes sense.

Hrútspungur (Iceland) I bet you thought Bjork was the craziest thing to come out of Iceland? Not even close. This dish consists of ram's testicles pickled in whey and pressed into little cakes. I take issue with this. I say, if you're gonna eat an animal's balls, be a man about it. Don't doctor it up and try to make it look fancy. Just cut the balls off, boil them, sprinkle them with salt and pepper, and have at it! Believe it or not, hrútspungur isn't even the oddest food in Iceland. That honor goes to . . .

Hakarl (Iceland) This dish can best be described by using three words that I was sure I'd never type in the same sentence. Fermented shark meat. The process goes like this: A large shark is cut up, buried in sand for many months, hung to let the powerful flavors develop, pressed, and then finally cut into small pieces. Then, the authorities come and haul your crazy Nordic ass off to the insane asylum. Or as it's called in Iceland, The Hakarl House. I love the fact that the sheer lunacy of the preparation obscures the fact that there are apparently sharks in Iceland.

Sannakji (Korea) Octopus. OK, world. We have a new player at the table, and they aren't fucking around. The Koreans will see your disgusting food, and raise you one tentacle. Yeah, yeah, yeah, I know what you're thinking. Every Tom, Dick and Harry has eaten calamari and maybe some of you have had the hrútspungurs to try octopus at a Japanese restaurant. But I doubt you've ever had them this way before. To prepare this dish, the chef slices off a tentacle of a live octopus and it's brought directly to your table. The tentacle goes down still squirming. I have two rules for my food. 1. It can't stink. 2. It can't fight back. When I sit down at the dinner table, I don't want anything on my plate to be able to put up a struggle.

Rat (China) I like this move by China. They are clearly subscribing to the Keep It Simple Stupid theory. Simple. Disgusting. Elegant.

Bird's Nest Soup (China) With over a billion people in their country, they're bound to have more than one freaky recipe, right? And I thought that black people were industrious for using the entire pig. Chinese people go so far as to use the nest of a swallow in this dish. Oddly, the actual swallow isn't used though. Some say that the nest isn't necessary to make this dish, but I disagree. Something about the twigs and bird saliva really makes this one special.

Balut (Philippines) Can't decide whether you want an egg or the full grown poultry that it would produce? Thanks to our friends from the Philippines, you don't have to choose. This traditional dish consists of a hard boiled, fertilized duck egg with a three week old embryo inside. Except a duck at three weeks looks more like a fetus than an embryo. (Not that an embryo is any more appetizing than a fetus, I'm just saying.) Balut is considered an aphrodisiac. All I can say on that is if Philipinos are turned on by eating duck fetus, they are some kinky bastards. I'm officially pro-life when it comes to ducks. Unless the mother duck's life is in danger. Or if she was raped. Fuck it. I guess a duck should have the right to choose.

Kutti Pi (India) (I swear I'm not making this shit up.) Let's keep the fetus theme going, shall we? In India, the Anglo-Indian population considers this dish a special treat for two reasons. One, it's extremely rare. It's only available if a pregnant animal just happens to be killed that day. (Or if you just happen to slip your butcher a few rupees.) Second, it's considered to have special medicinal properties for pregnant women and people with tuberculosis or back pain. What could be better for the health and karma of a mother to be, than eating the unborn child of another species?

We can say that a particular black person isn't black enough. You can't. There are subtle nuances to blackness that your untrained Caucasian eyes can't possibly pick up. Take Ed Bradley for example. Older, articulate, conservative in manner . . . very black. Maybe it's the wardrobe. He refuses to make his look completely "understated journalist." He keeps just a smidge of hipness to his clothes. It could be the earring that adds just a dash of pimp to his overall appearance. You just know that if he has one too many glasses of cognac at the CBS Christmas party, he's liable to curse someone out. Can't you just see him in an argument? "Oh I'm sorry. You're right. I mean, you should know. You are a big-time, Emmy award-winning journalist and all. No, wait. That's me. Those are *my* eleven Emmy awards, not yours. You're Janice from the legal department who, to the best of my knowledge, has never won so much as a fucking Peabody! Bitch, I'm Ed motherfucking Bradley! How many niggers you know can say they kept it real in Saigon?"

Truth be told, there should probably be some sort of scale on which to rate your degree of ethnicity. Sort of a Richter scale to measure how black or Latin or Asian you are. That way, white people could have an idea what they're getting themselves into. When a white woman comes home and tells her parents that she's dating a Mexican guy, they won't freak out. "Mom, Dad . . . he's only a 4.8 on the ethnicity scale! He's not like Cheech from *Cheech and Chong*; he's more like Cheech from *Nash Bridges*. Totally harmless."

I think I'd fall at about a 6.7 on this scale. Not anywhere near Spike Lee, but quite a few notches higher than Cuba Gooding Jr. I'm representing. Somewhat. I'm a reasonable representative. I'm keeping it real . . . istic. Realistic. Not so much real, as based on real life events. I'm kind of a like a one man episode of *Law & Order*. Although, I'm not sure how black I can be. I don't eat watermelon and I don't drink iced tea. I used to go to our family reunions and just stand there.

Young white males. Be yourself. Pull up your pants, turn your baseball caps around, and stop trying to be black. And stop wearing our clothes. Here's a hint: "FUBU" means For Us By Us. Act accordingly. (Although FUBU now has both stores and wholesale distribution in Korea and Japan. Somehow, For Them By Us just doesn't have the same ring to it.) Why would you want to dress black anyway? Being black is still a tremendous disadvantage in this country. Black people live in poorer homes, make less money, get inferior health care, and die at a younger age than white people. Why would you want to be associated with that if you didn't have to be? Pretty soon looking and acting black isn't going to be enough of a disadvantage for these young Eminem wannabes. They're going to be acting handicapped too. They'll be limping around the mall with their homeboys.

"Yeah dog, I know you ain't never noticed my club foot before, but it's not like I have an actual physical club foot per se.

40

Nah, what I have is more of a spiritual emotional clubfoot. Know what I'm saying? My soul is handicapped, dog."

It's amazing to think of the lesson that society has taught these kids. They've seen so many rap music videos and watched so much professional sports that they've convinced themselves that being black is somehow much more fun than being white. Sure it is. High blood pressure, police brutality, racial profiling, disenfranchisement—black people are having a ball! Josh, Brett, Ethan . . . put down those voter registration cards and join the fun!

Being black isn't nearly as fun as it used to be. For one thing, white people aren't as scared of us as they used to be. I guess when there's a chance that an Al Qaeda member might be planning on blowing up your next flight, you're really not going to be that intimidated when Tyrell tries to cut in line at the DMV.

Chapter 5

Once You Go Black . . .
All Hell Breaks Loose

For the black man, dating white women is risky business. Not for all the obvious reasons that most people think of, e.g., family and societal backlash. It's just that there are too many expectations. White women have spent their entire lives hearing about the alleged monstrosity that lurks between the thighs of black men. It's a legend on par with the Loch Ness monster, Bigfoot, The Lost City of Atlantis, or George W. Bush's service in the Texas Air National Guard. It's stressful enough just dealing with the early stages of a relationship without having that extra-added penis pressure put on you. I'm 5 feet 11 inches tall, which is slightly above average for an American man. I'm pretty sure those proportions hold for all of my various body parts. I can't live up to the hype. But hey, I can run fast and jump high. Two out of three ain't bad.

People always like to talk about the black man's supposedly unquenchable thirst for blond hair and blue eyes. I will be the first to admit that most of the brothers I've known in my life have been at least a little curious. But if pressed to describe their ideal mate or sex partner, I would be willing to bet my life that most black men would paint a picture of someone much closer to Pam Grier or Salma Hayek than to Gwyneth Paltrow or Britney Spears.

I have no evidence to back up my next claim. I'll be the first person to admit that I have nothing to base this on but my own pop psychology, gut instinct, and discussions with other black men. White women think that they are more attractive to black men than they really are. The average adult has a pretty good sense of their appearance. They know how attractive they are, and more importantly, how attractive they are not. When I'm well groomed and well dressed, I feel confident that I can walk into a bar, restaurant, nightclub, or party and make a pretty good impression on people of the opposite sex, and maybe even some members of my own sex. I don't have any illusions of turning every head when I walk in the room, and I don't carry myself as if I do. We've all seen people who seem to think much too highly of themselves.

In my experience, when white women are around black men, a lot of them seem to think this way. It's incredibly subtle and in- tuitive, but I'm convinced it's real. There seems to be this energy emitting from them that says, "Well, if I were to give him the time of day, he'd have to consider himself lucky." There have been situations where I have actually gotten offended that a white woman expressed interest in me or flirted with me. "I'm supposed to sweat her just because she's white? Who in the hell does she think she is? I'm *much* more attractive than she is!" This attitude probably comes from growing up in households where they were socialized to believe blacks inferior.

I can't help but think that some of that attitude still lingers in the hearts and minds of many white women today. Even though they may not carry any overt prejudice in their hearts, deep down they still think that any black man who spends time with them is somehow elevating his station. And why shouldn't they think they're hot shit? White women have been put up on a pedestal for generations. Their entire standard of beauty dominates popular culture.

Quick! What was the first thing the stylists did to Mariah Carey, Jennifer Lopez, and Beyoncé once they started blowing up? They lightened their hair. I guess Americans can appreciate the more sturdy legs and curvier backside of the ethnic woman. But if you want to be thought of as a pretty pop star, you have to be blond. Or Pink. But she's not so much pretty as she is scary. I think I would make out with Pink at a club just because I'd probably be too intimidated by her to say no if she put the moves on me. I'd make out with her, but I wouldn't date her. I couldn't date any woman who looks tougher in a wife beater and jeans than I do. She straddles that border between masculine and feminine better than anyone since Brigitte Neilsen.

When I was in high school in North Carolina, I developed a close friendship with a white girl who was a year older than I was. What started out as an innocent, purely platonic friendship based on our mutual appreciation of a De La Soul album, quickly blossomed into good old-fashioned puppy love. We clearly liked each other, but because of the racial climate in my town, nothing ever developed. We only talked openly about our situation once. During that conversation, she confessed her feelings to me, but admitted that nothing could ever happen between us because her parents would go crazy. Although I was obviously hurt, I couldn't help being more than a little bit angry as well. I was more popular than she was, I was more intelligent than she was, I was considered more attractive than she was, and I ended up going to a better college than she did. How dare her family think that I'm somehow beneath their daughter?

Hey, Mr. and Mrs. Farmer. I wrote a book. Suck on that for a while.

The confusing thing about this kind of behavior is that white women are just as curious, just as eager to experiment—if not more—as black men are. Each fall, all across the country, white girls everywhere show up to college campuses looking for the biggest thighs and the largest feet they can spot. As soon as their parents have headed back home, a segment of every white, female, freshman class begins scouring the quad for anything dark that they can get their hands on. Football players, basketball players, licorice, Magic Markers; anything black will do. In my freshman year at Wake Forest University, half of the janitorial staff went to winter formals. And why not? College is the perfect time for them to experiment. When you're in high school, you have to deal with your close-minded friends and family. Not to mention, no white woman wants to look back at her senior prom picture and see some guy in a high top fade, or some cornrows. The hairstyles of teenage black males don't tend to age very well. After college, it's time to get serious about finding a mate. Even though the numbers of black/white interracial marriages are on the rise, the truth is that most white women are still reticent about spending their early motherhood years taming a mass of wild, frizzy hair. Every time I see a white mother walking with her obviously biracial children I want to give them a coupon to the best beauty salon on the south side of whatever town it is that I'm in. For god sakes, is it that hard to learn how to plait your little girl's hair? But I digress.

Not that I didn't do my fair share of experimenting during my four years of college. But I did attend a liberal arts school. Very liberal. You had to date a white girl if you wanted to graduate. It was mandatory. So, I threw myself headfirst into the core curriculum by dating the whitest girl I could find. Her name was Kate, and she was a blond field hockey player from Connecticut. She had never heard of A Tribe Called Quest. She would wear a Jägermeister cowboy hat when she drank. She would get confused if I called my roommate by any of the dozen terms of affection that black men have for each other. "I thought you told me your roommate's name was Mike, why did you just call him Joe?"

For all of our differences, I can honestly say that race was very rarely a factor in our relationship. Oddly enough, her name often posed more of a challenge than her skin color. At a predominantly white university, there are bound to be several dozen Kates on campus. Of course most of them were only acquaintances to us and we never really knew their last names. So, we devised a system of Kate recognition that proved to be quite useful. All the other Kates that we knew were categorized not by last name, but by campus affiliation or some sort of identifying experience that we had with them. The Kate that I was seeing was Nick's Kate, or field-hockey Kate. There was also Kate-with-the-big-ass Kate. That one is pretty self-explanatory. Although I once had to explain to her friend—also named Kate—that we meant it as a compliment. There was Nuh Nuh Nuh Kate. She was the friend who needed the explanation. We called her "Nuh Nuh Nuh" because during a hook up with our friend Rob, she was too drunk to even tell him no. She could only manage, "Nuh. Nuh. Nuh." Don't worry. He was a total gentleman. Except for the fact that a gentleman would never have told his friends that story. There was urinator Kate, who got drunk and peed in my best friend's suitcase. It sounds like a real hassle, but he got a brand new set of Tumi luggage out of it. There was track Kate who once made the following comment about grits, "I've heard they're good. I'd like to try one sometime." I probably laughed for five minutes straight before I could get myself under control enough to explain to her the problem with eating a single grit.

The only times the racial difference reared its ugly head was when we both ended up at Corbin's, the local college bar. Everyone went there on Thursday nights for $1.00 longnecks of domestic beer and cheesy dance music. If you were fortunate, you could witness one of the funniest phenomena of the black male/white female dating scenario. If I was unfortunate, I could have been the one that you were laughing at. Here's how it works. Black guy and white girl are dating, hooking up on a regular basis or just happen to be flirting seriously on this particular night. Odds are that they'll be going home together. The happy couple is grinding away on the dance floor as Tone Loc bleats his way through "Wild Thing." On the periphery of the floor, the other black men in the bar sense what's coming next. By the time he realizes what he's done . . . it's too late.

Sidebar. One of the great things about Corbin's was that they played the exact same tape every Thursday night. Same songs, same order. Like clockwork. It doesn't sound like much, but you would be surprised how much this enhanced the Thursday night experience. For example, when we got to the bar, I knew exactly how much time I had to drink before the serious dancing began. Once Shannon's "Let the Music Play" started, I knew I was going to be on the floor for about forty-five minutes nonstop. Also, I knew not to enjoy dancing to The Jackson Five's "ABC" too much because "I Will Survive" came right after that. Once that song is played, every man in the building might as well cease to exist. Spontaneous circles of five, six or seven women pop up all over the dance floor with whichever young lady has been done wrong most recently screaming at the top of her lungs, "I don't need you Brad! I've got all my life to live!" I curse the day that song was recorded. A pox on your house, Gloria Gaynor.

But back to our happy couple. What is forgotten is that immediately following "Wild Thing" is the Lynyrd Skynyrd white trash anthem, "Sweet Home Alabama." Here I am, trying to enjoy the fruits of the white man's tree without losing my Afrocentricity. Without being labeled a sell-out. The next thing I know, the heartfelt vocals of Ronnie Van Zant and the incendiary guitar playing of Gary Rossington have transformed Kate into a tube top-wearing, Pall Mall-chain-smoking, Pabst Blue Ribbon-chugging wild woman. Remember, this is a girl from Connecticut. That's the power of that song. Sure, I'll dance with a white woman, but I ain't dancing with no fucking redneck. It's the ultimate test of how much you want to spend the evening with a white woman. Well, maybe not the ultimate test. Once Kate wanted me to watch *Melrose Place* with her. As I was sitting there, with my arm around her watching the trashy trials and tribulations of Michael, Jane, Allison & Billy, I realized that I had gone too far astray from my people. There was only one way to counteract the whitest moment of my life; with the blackest moment of my life. I immediately put on a FUBU jersey, went outside to the basketball courts, and slam-dunked a watermelon.

Once during my junior year, a white classmate of mine told me, "I don't believe in interracial dating." Not that he didn't agree with it. Not that he thought it was a bad idea given all of the problems that it could cause those involved. No, he used the word "believe." I laughed in his face. "What, do you refuse to accept that it exists? It's not like the tooth fairy or Santa Claus. Believe me, it's real. I'm going over to the Kappa Kappa Gamma house right now and Susan Yelverton is taking me to the movies. Later on this evening, I hope to be ejaculating somewhere in her vicinity. This isn't like those elusive lipstick lesbians everyone hears about but never actually sees. Whether you believe it or not, black men are fucking white women right now." I try to use the phrase "fucking white women" from time to time. Just because I know it makes white people uncomfortable. Except for the percentage of white women reading this book who are wondering if all that "I don't have a huge dick" stuff was just a joke. Those ladies aren't uncomfortable at all right now. For the record, it was a joke. I'm hung like a fucking rhinoceros.

But I don't have to worry about any of this now because I'm married and I'm pretty sure my wife would frown upon me dating white women. My wife is Native American, but she doesn't fit the stereotypical view of what an Indian person looks like. My father-in-law is Alaskan native and therefore he's not incredibly dark-skinned. My mother-in-law's father was white, so her skin tone is fair for an Indian as well. As a result, people have absolutely no idea what my wife is when they meet her. I know it's annoying for her to deal with, but I enjoy watching her play this game of ethnic 20 questions.

"So . . . where are you from?"

"I grew up mostly in the Seattle area."

"And before that?"

"Umm, Alaska."

"Right. But where are you from originally?"

"Before Alaska? The womb."

"Yeah. Is there any history of diabetes or sickle cell anemia in your family?"

It's right about here that she gets fed up and just tells people that she's Indian. Mostly people just want to talk her face off about how much they love turquoise and how their grandmother was half Cherokee. She gets sick of having these conversations, but I have to deal with my own set of questions based on her ethnicity. The first thing people want to ask me is, "What's it like being with someone who's Indian?" What's it like? I never know what people expect me to say to that. It's not like she attacks me with a tomahawk if I come home late. It's just a normal, healthy marriage like anyone else's. Of course, there are some traditions that we have to observe. For example every Columbus Day I have to rape her and then give her a blanket that's infected with small pox. I know it sounds harsh, but who am I to question her culture? The good thing about our relationship is that it comes with a built-in excuse. If we can't make the marriage work, we'll just blame whitey. Chances are, with our combined legacy of racial suffering, white people did something along the way to cause our breakup anyway.

One of the most persistent statements that is directed toward my wife and me is the assumption that we're going to have really attractive children. For some reason, people believe that the genes of different racial groups always combine to form some sort of olive-skinned, brown-haired wonder child. Since I have eyes and more than a rudimentary grasp of basic genetics, I know that this isn't always the case. I've gotten so sick and tired of hearing these comments that I'm starting to hope that my wife and I have at least one ugly child just so that I can make my point. I think the best case scenario would see us having a son that looks like The Rock, a daughter that looks like Rosario Dawson, and then another son who looks just a little bit like Carrot Top so I can say, "See! I told you!" He could have little kiddie props and he could entertain the other kids in kindergarten before naptime. And then, when he becomes a rebellious, teenaged prop comic, he and I will reach an unavoidable *Great Santini*-like impasse and I'll declare, "I have no son!" Of course, I say that only in jest. I can't think of anything that would terrify me more than seeing my wife give birth to a tiny little Carrot Top. As if the idea of an eight-pound creature emerging from my wife's vagina isn't scary enough, let's give him bright red, frizzy hair, freckles, and weird eyebrows to make the nightmare even worse.

The children of interracial couples have become the lightning rod for debate in recent years. Since it's no longer socially acceptable to be against dating outside of one's race just because, the closed minded among us have now taken up the position that their only concern is for the children.

"I don't care who you want to marry, I'm just worried about the children. They aren't going to be black. They aren't going to be Native American. What are they going to be, Nick?"

What are they going to be? I'll tell you what my children are going to be. They're going to be loved, they're going to be doted upon, they're going to be nurtured, and they're going to be supported in every way possible. My children are going to *be* black and Native American, which means they're going to *be* able to get into any college or university in the country, so spare me that thinly veiled racist garbage. Black and Native American? Are you kidding me? Every forward-thinking admissions officer in the country is going to be bending over backward to bring in children like ours.

"Hi, Malik Running Cloud? This is Jim Wheeler over here at Bleeding Heart University. I just wanted to call you personally and let you know that we'd love to see you on campus in the fall."

PART III

Music and
Culture

Chapter 6

Eminem: Latest in a Long Line of Saviors

For the past twenty-five years, hip-hop music has been lost. An entire generation of black males has spent their formative years wandering around aimlessly. Trapped in a maze of turntables, speakers, and cross faders. Then, at long last, a pale rider materializes on the horizon. Like a modern-day Tarzan, he swings through the urban jungle on his microphone cord teaching the natives how to negotiate the mean streets and express themselves poetically. Thank God he finally came and showed us the way.

A little over the top, huh? Well, that's basically what the media has been feeding us about Eminem since he exploded onto the scene in 1999. Think about it. Is it just a coincidence that the rap artist who has received the most critical praise, sold the most albums, and won the most awards just happens to be white? Of course it isn't. Here's what the American public has told us when it comes to Eminem: "I know black people have been doing this particular genre of music for a long time. Forget about Kurtis Blow, RUN-DMC, LL Cool J, Rakim, Chuck D, KRS-One, Tupac, Notorious B.I.G., Nas, Common, Mos Def . . . those guys are all OK. But I really think this white guy is on to something here."

Somewhere, Little Richard and Chuck Berry are watching TV and thinking, "Here we go again."

I'm not saying that he isn't talented. He's clearly a gifted MC, annoying little brother voice aside. I just have a hard time believing that he's any more gifted than the rappers that I named earlier. Or a dozen or so others for that matter. I had this argument with a white friend and he tried to sell me the line about how creative and visionary Eminem is and how no other rappers have done the kinds of things he's done in songs before. To bolster his argument, he used the song "Stan." Over an incredibly haunting track—lifted from pop star Dido—Eminem's lyrics take the form of letters exchanged between himself and an obsessed fan, Stan. It's a clever and memorable tune. But it isn't groundbreaking. The entire time he was making his case, I just smiled politely. My repertoire of music knowledge includes more than Steely Dan. When he was done talking, I politely, calmly, embarrassed the hell out of him. I told him the following things.

On their 1993 debut *Reachin'*, the group Digable Planets addressed the abortion issue with their song "La Femme Fetal." The song finds one of the members—who is male—telling the story of his friend's anguish over her decision to have an abortion. He recounts their conversation in vivid, poetic lyrics that elevate music to the level of sociopolitical discourse.

It was a perfect example of what hip-hop could be. Even though everyone from my generation knows all of the words to their most popular song *Rebirth of Slick*, most people don't even remember this track.

In 1996, Nas released his second album, *It Was Written*. Nas had come out of nowhere with his landmark debut, *Illmatic*, two years earlier and everyone was eager to see what he was going to come up with next. The first time I heard the track "I Gave You Power," my jaw dropped. Written from the perspective of a handgun, the song does more to explain the phenomenon of inner city shootings in a few minutes than a lifetime of documentaries, panel discussions, and Senate hearings ever could. The chorus of the song still gives me goose bumps.

At the end of the song, the owner of the gun gets shot dead. As bystanders run away from the scene, someone else grabs the gun and takes off into the night.

In 1991, De La Soul released the follow-up to their groundbreaking debut *3 Feet High and Rising*. Seeking to bury their image as peace-loving hippies, they titled the album *De La Soul is Dead*. Halfway through the album comes one of my all-time favorite De La tunes, "Millie Pulled a Pistol on Santa." "Millie" tells the story of a teenage girl who is being sexually and physically abused by her father. When she reaches out to her friends and tells them of the abuse, they're reluctant to believe her because her father also happens to be an extremely popular counselor at their school, taking the kids on roller skating trips and playing Santa Claus at Macy's. Fed up, Millie decides to get a gun and end the torture the only way she knows how. She walks into the crowded department store, pulls out a gun, and shoots her father.

When I was finished with my impromptu hip-hop dissertation, I told my friend, "Eminem is not reinventing the wheel. He's not elevating the genre to previously unseen heights. He's just white." He mumbled something about the new Nelly album and walked off.

The thing that angers me the most is the ridiculous double standard that is being applied. The same critics who questioned

Tupac's misogynist lyrics have no problem listening to Eminem describe his desire to kill both his mother and his ex-wife. The same fans that were turned off by Notorious B.I.G.'s detailed accounts of drug deals and shoot-outs don't have any such qualms about listening to Eminem spit similar lyrics about society's underbelly. The same law enforcement officials who arrested members of 2 Live Crew for rapping about explicit sexual behavior showed no interest in locking Eminem up for his explicit gay-bashing lyrics. We're talking about a guy who wrote openly about his hatred of "fags" and stabbing them in the head. Often when people use language like that they attempt to diffuse criticism by suggesting that they are simply referring to "fags" to mean men who aren't tough, or someone who's being a sissy. But Eminem distinctly names homosexuals, transvestites and oddly enough hemaphrodites in his lyrics. Honestly, have hermphrodites ever really hurt anybody? Frankly I've never understood this kind of homophobia. While we're on the subject of homophobia, will you please allow me a brief diatribe on the matter? (What am I talking about? Of course you'll allow it. You bought the book didn't you?) My confusion isn't with the concept of homophobia. I think all reasonable people who aren't morons or Republican Senators from Pennsylvania can agree that anger or hatred towards someone just because of their sexual orientation is just plain wrong. My problem is with the term itself. Homophobia. A phobia is a fear. I don't think anyone is actually *afraid* of gay people. I've spent most of my adult life living in the West Hollywood section of Los Angeles; one of the most gay friendly neighborhoods in America. I've been around a fair amount of homosexual men and women in my life. I think it's safe to say that I've never once been afraid around gay people. Even when I was hit on by a 6-foot 4-inch tall drag queen in a green chiffon ball gown in a bar in Chicago—long story, maybe in the next book—I wasn't really afraid. Uncomfortable? Yes. Flattered? Yes. Afraid? Absolutely not. In fact, the list of things that I'm actually afraid of stops at just two. One, Cirque du Soleil. (I can't explain it. Something about that stuff just really, really creeps me the fuck out.) Two, the flying monkeys from the original *Wizard of Oz*.

Of course, when people use the term homophobia, it doesn't mean an actual fear of gay people. What it really means is that person, in this case Eminem, clearly has a violent distaste for man on man action. As a straight guy, I can understand being kind of repulsed by the idea of having another man's penis in the vicinity of any of my orifices. It's just not my cup of tea. But you know what? I don't have to worry about that happening either. Unless I go to prison or pass out naked, face down, ass up on the middle of the sidewalk in the Castro district of San Francisco, with a huge bottle of lube laying right next to me, I don't have to worry about being involved in any homosexual activity. It just isn't a concern. So, I don't rail against people who have a different sexual proclivity than I do. And since their sexual activities don't impact my life in any way, I don't call them names, or put them down, or ask them to hide their behavior or decry their desire to be legally married. I just leave them alone to suck and fuck with impunity in all of their homosexual glory.

Also, Eminem is a rock star. I'm sure beautiful women of all shapes and sizes are throwing themselves at him constantly. We're talking about an institution that allows painfully unattractive men like Rick Ocasek and Lyle Lovett to sleep with and even marry women like Paulina Porizkova and Julia Roberts. Why is gay sex even in his mind at all? If I was a young, single heterosexual male rock star every waking moment of my day would revolve around two things: song lyrics and vaginas. I would write lyrics about vaginas. I would declare Playmate Tuesdays, and on those days I would have sex with a bona fide Playboy playmate; flying her in if need be. (Barbie Benton, I'm looking at you.) I would hire a personal assistant who's job would be just to keep track of the various actresses, super models and pop or R&B starlets that I was banging. I would purchase the original Princess Leia costume and make my dates wear it out in public. The ways in which I could occupy myself with heterosexual activity are endless. But this dummy is too busy penning his scurrilous screed against hermaphrodites. Could it be that Mr. Mathers is covering up a deeper issue? I'm not saying Eminem is gay, but you know how the old saying goes: If it walks like a duck, and quacks like a duck . . . Eminem is gay.

And Elton John still saw fit to perform a duet with him at the Grammy's? Actually, Elton has been one of Eminem's biggest defenders. He's been quoted as saying, "There is far more humor on the album than people think. It appeals to my English black sense of humor." Humor? Well, if he liked that, I've got a joke that I'm sure Elton John will love.

A faggot walks into a bar with a duck on his head.

The bull dyke bartender says to the sissy, "Can I help you, you peter puffer?"

The duck says, "Yeah, get this fairy off my ass, you muff diver!"

Hilarious, huh Elton? Seriously though, I thought you had to be black to be an Uncle Tom. Obviously, Elton John's desire to remain in the public eye and try to sell albums overrode his self-respect. So much so that he got down on his knees on national television and sucked the huge, erect cock of publicity. No disrespect to his sexual orientation, but here is a guy who has spent his adult life being openly and proudly gay—which is a beautiful thing—but then an obvious insult to his sexuality appears in the form of a platinum recording artist, and he just ignores it?

I can't wait to see the performance where Elton John takes the stage with Brand Nubian to help them perform their songs "Pass the Gat" and "Punks Jump Up to Get Beat Down" where they say things like "shoot the faggot in the back for acting like that" and "fuck up a faggot . . . don't understand their ways and I ain't down with gays." Wouldn't you love to see Elton crooning with Jamaican dance hall legend Buju Banton on his classic "Boom Bye Bye?" After all, the lyric "it's like/Boom bye bye, in a batty boy head, rude boy no promote no nasty man, them hafi dead" translates into: "bang-bang, in a faggot's head/Homeboys don't condone nasty men/They must die." Buju's people will be expecting your call any day now, Elton.

Maybe Elton was trying to usher in a new age of contradictory duets? There are dozens of amazing possibilities if the artists involved would only put aside their differences. Perhaps we'll see Ike and Tina Turner do a reunion concert. The stage dynamic would probably suffer from the 500 yard buffer required by the restraining order, but "Proud Mary" would still rock, damn it. I think a Neil Young/Lynyrd Skynyrd double bill is feasible as long as there isn't any Jack Daniels or Jim Beam in the entire building. One time only, pay-per-view special. Britney Spears, Christina Aguilera and Pink. They could all bury the hatchet for a concert to be followed immediately by hard-core lesbian porn. I would pay to see that and so would you.

To illustrate the double standard that applies to Eminem, let us examine what happened with the 2004 Video Music Awards on MTV. Jamaican dancehall star Beenie Man was scheduled to perform at a concert associated with the awards show. As I illustrated earlier, dance hall is known for sometimes violently anti-gay lyrics and Beenie Man has boasted on his songs "I'm dreaming of a new Jamaica, come to execute all the gays" and "Queers must be killed." A Miami-based gay rights group announced plans to protest the concert and MTV quickly dropped Beenie Man from the show's roster saying, "We don't want anything to overshadow what will be a great weekend of music events for South Floridians." Oh, I see how it works. When a black guy bashes gays, it distracts from the weekend of music events. When a white guy bashes gays, it *is* the event. The threat of the protests and his subsequent removal from the show is made slightly curious by the fact that Beenie Man had issued an apology for the lyrics in some of his earlier songs like "Bad Man Chi Chi Man (Bad Man, Queer Man)." His statement read as follows:

"Certain lyrics and recordings I have made in the past may have caused distress and outrage among people whose identities and lifestyles are different from my own. . . . I offer my sincerest apologies to those who might have been offended, threatened or hurt by my songs."

Wow. That sounds like a guy who either truly regrets the things that he said in the past, or at least has the brains to realize that you can't say ignorant violent shit on wax without having it come back to bite you in the ass. Or, maybe he's just a guy who knows that MTV isn't committed to making him a huge star no matter how much ignorant shit he says.

As if over-hyping Eminem's musical talents wasn't enough, the media also went and made him a movie star. Curtis Hanson—the man behind the camera for the near perfect *L.A. Confi-*

dential—brought Eminem's story to the screen in 2002's *8 Mile.* The movie was a critical and commercial success. Obviously, there have been movies about hip-hop before. (Although it's tough to call *Breakin' 2: Electric Boogaloo* a movie. But, technically, it fits the criteria.) But why did it take twenty years and a white rapper for someone of Curtis Hanson's caliber to bring a semi-autobiographical hip-hop story to the screen in such a big way? Perhaps there was a lack of intriguing, compelling stories to tell?

Well, someone could have told the story of KRS-One. Born Kris Parker, he left his mother's home in the Bronx at fourteen and spent the next six years living on the streets and in various homeless shelters. He tried to continue his education by studying in public libraries. During this time, he began writing rhymes and tagging graffiti with his nickname KRS-One. After doing jail time for selling marijuana, he met social worker Scott Sterling in a Bronx shelter in 1985. The two struck up a friendship over their mutual love of hip-hop. Sterling was also a DJ who went by the name Scott La Rock. They decided to form the group Boogie Down Productions. Their debut album, *Criminal Minded*, earned them a rabid following and is considered a classic of the genre. The record's success attracted the attention of RCA affiliate Jive Records, and the duo signed a record contract. Not long afterward, Scott La Rock was attempting to break up a fight at a party and was shot and killed. Saddened by the loss of his friend, KRS-One decided to continue working on the second album, and in 1988, *By Any Means Necessary* was released. Calling himself "the teacher" he focused his lyrics on aggressive, sometimes militant social commentary. Widely regarded as the first "conscious rapper," KRS-One still continues to record, tour, and speak all over the country.

Or you could tell the story of Tupac Shakur. Born in jail to a former Black Panther. Goes on to be a successful rapper and actor before dying in a hail of gunfire. To this day, some insist that he faked his own death and several posthumously released albums do nothing to dispel those rumors. Or you could tell the story of Christopher Wallace, a.k.a. Biggie Smalls, a.k.a. Notorious B.I.G. Small-time drug dealer turns successful rap star, only to be gunned down. Some say his murder was in retaliation for Shakur's killing. There was also a documentary produced by an award-winning filmmaker that suggests that the Los Angeles Police Department was implicated in both murders. Is that enough drama for you, Hollywood? Or maybe that's too much drama for white America to take. How about we turn the Biggie/Tupac story into a slapstick comedy staring Marlon Wayans and Anthony Anderson?

But let's be honest. We all know why no Oscar-winning directors are scrambling to make the KRS-One story, or the Tupac story, or the Biggie story. They aren't white. This isn't anything new. There is a long, rich tradition in Hollywood—and America—of ignoring social issues and entire cultures until they effect or relate to white people. The origin of mankind can be traced to the continent of Africa. So, it's safe to say that the tribes there have a pretty good handle on the way things go down in the jungle, right? What did white people do? They wrote books and produced movies about a white man who is raised in Africa and can swing through the trees and talk to the animals. Meanwhile, entire villages of natives are running around like some African version of the Keystone Cops. I can actually remember the day when the hypocrisy of all this dawned on me. There I was on a Sunday afternoon watching Johnny Weissmuller do his thing when the lightbulb went off, "Wait a minute. Why can't any of the African guys do this shit? Man . . . fuck Tarzan!"

In a post-Civil War frontier setting, I'm sure there are hundreds of amazing Native American stories that could be told. What did Hollywood do? While an entire race of people is almost being wiped off the face of the Earth, they focus on a white man and a white woman's problems, and Kevin Costner gets an Oscar for *Dances With Wolves*. I don't care what anyone says, I hate that damned movie and I don't ever want to watch it again. Unless they release a special edition DVD where Lt. John Dunbar gets smallpox and dies in the first twenty minutes. Someone get the folks at Criterion on the phone. And I love how they conveniently placed an older white woman in the Indian tribe so Costner could have a white love interest. Right. He's surrounded by dozens of beautiful, nubile Sioux women with cascading hair, and he falls for the older white lady. That's real believable.

Tom Cruise as a samurai? Call me crazy, but I don't think any self-respecting samurai would ever be caught dead with that smug grin on his face. And if he were, I'm pretty sure that he would have been forced to perform seppuku on the spot. *The Last Samurai*—or *Dances With Swords*, as my wife likes to call it—is annoying as a concept, not just because it's the latest in a long line of "white guy saves minority" films. It's also the latest in a long line of unofficial *Top Gun* rip-offs that Mr. Cruise has bestowed on us.

☞ **1986. *The Color of Money.*** *Top Gun* in a pool hall. Nice hair Tom. Paul Newman looks lost and confused for the duration. You know a movie is doomed when it's trying to make something that is fundamentally not cool to watch in person cool to pay $8.50 to watch in a movie theater. I really hate this movie, but I have to give them bonus points for using that Warren Zevon werewolf song. *Owoooooooooo!!!*

☞ **1988.** *Cocktail.* *Top Gun* in a bar. The tag line for the movie was, "When he pours, he reigns." I'm not making that up. I am neither clever nor retarded enough to come up with anything like that. Sadly, the tag line is funnier and more interesting than anything in the actual movie. They get bonus points for having Elizabeth Shue and Gina Gershon in the film, but I can't understand how a movie can have those two in it and still not keep my interest. Amazing. How many bartenders across the country got punched in the mouth because they spilled Jack Daniels all over some guy while twirling the bottle around like some sort of bartending majorette? The answer? 47. I looked it up. Just pour the drinks, dude.

☞ **1990.** *Days of Thunder.* *Top Gun* on a racetrack. Let's play a game. It's called try and guess what drug they were doing when they came up with the idea for this one. It couldn't have been pot because the movie isn't funny. It couldn't have been coke because the story is way too thin. A cokehead would have stayed up all night coming up with some longwinded elaborate back-story with a Shyamalan-esque twist at the end. I think the producers of this film were doing heroin. Right before they shot up, one guy said to the other, "We could just do *Top Gun* in a NASCAR setting."

"Good idea dude. Let's flesh the story out. Pass me that needle."

Then, they both nodded off and slept right up until the pitch meeting. They get some bonus points for naming the lead character Cole Trickle though.

☞ **1992. *A Few Good Men.*** Yeah, I know it was a well-received movie, and I actually enjoyed it. But that doesn't change the fact that it was *Top Gun* in a courtroom. It makes you wonder what might have happened if Aaron Sorkin had written *Days of Thunder* or Jack Nicholson had been the other bartender in *Cocktail* doesn't it?

"You can't handle the Cuervo!!!"

They get bonus points for putting Demi Moore in the tight-fighting military uniform. Yes, I know she was fully clothed the entire time, but she's *that* hot.

☞ **1996. *Jerry Maguire.*** *Top Gun* as a sports agent. Wait, a maverick sports agent? OK, I tried to give my man Cameron Crowe the benefit of the doubt. He's earned it from me. But I still hate this movie. The fact that he had a hand in *Fast Times at Ridgemont High, Say Anything,* and *Almost Famous*—three of my favorite movies of all time—is the only thing stopping me from going to his home and seriously whupping his ass for unleashing the phrase "show me the money" on our culture. Besides, you can't take a movie about a sports agent and turn it into a chick flick. That's just wrong. Bonus points for shooting the climactic scene where the Cardinals beat my beloved Dallas Cowboys in the big game. Because we all know that never happens in real life.

But back to the white savior syndrome. It's been around a long time. It's going to be around for a long time to come. But don't expect me to sit by and watch you co-opt other people's cultures and tell us you've improved on them without me calling you out on it. This leads me back to Eminem. If you want to believe that he's the greatest rapper of all time, go right ahead. If you want to believe that all the violent, ignorant, misogynist drivel he spews out is somehow misunderstood genius, go right ahead. If you want to believe that the most praised rapper in the history of the genre just *happens* to be white, go right ahead. But please, don't blow that smoke up my ass.

The white savior phenomenon is just one of the inevitable repercussions that are the result of the gentrification of hip-hop music. Black folks have been complaining about the co-opting of our culture for years now. But it seems to have reached a fever pitch during the last five years. Rappers like DMX and Ludacris would have been relegated to appearing only on BET a few years ago. Now, they make appearances on MTV's *TRL* and are greeted with the same zealous fanfare as *NSYNC or Britney Spears. Snoop Dogg materialized onto the music scene on the murky hit, *Deep Cover*. His lazy delivery, lanky, squinty-eyed appearance and casual demeanor helped him to carve his niche in the industry. Snoop was like the second cousin or great uncle that you met once or twice at a family reunion. No one ever really knew exactly what he was into, but everyone knew that it wasn't exactly legal. Now, look at him. Appearing in the *Starsky & Hutch* movie as a lame, warmed over version of Huggy Bear, and shilling for AOL in television commercials. I think the exact death of hip-hop music can be traced to the second that Snoop uttered the line, "Now wait just one minizzle." Is this the same Long Beach gang banger that once rapped about killing policemen and selling drugs? This is the kind of thing that makes me want to hop into a DeLorean, fire up the flux capacitor, and go back in time to the Bronx of the 1970s . . . and shoot Kool Herc in the head. Pretty soon, I'm going to have to seriously consider just abandoning hip-hop altogether. Maybe I'll just immerse myself in some obscure genre of music that mainstream America totally ignores.

"So, Nick. What did you get into this weekend?"

"Awww man. We went down to that Polka club on 3rd Street last night."

"How was it?"

"It was hot. Walter Ostanek was in town. That nigger was spitting hot fire out of the accordion!"

I'm not annoyed because white people like rap music. I'm not even annoyed because white people like horrible rap music. I'm annoyed because white people take horrible rap music, play it on the radio and on MTV all day every day, and then completely ignore the good stuff. A white person buying a rap album at a record store is just like me ordering wine in a restaurant. I have absolutely no idea what I'm doing, and it shows. The waiter brings out the bottle and pours me that first sip to sample. I taste it, hold it in my mouth for what seems like long enough for anyone who knows something about wine to make a decision, and then I go, "This is fine." So, most white people just end up buying the house wine, which usually sucks. Anything that doesn't promote what America's narrow-minded idea of what black men are supposed to be gets left behind in the bargain bin at Tower Records while the new Nelly album flies off the shelf. Why is it that a white rock group like Weezer or The Strokes can shoot a video where they just stand there in their T-shirts and sweaters and play their instruments and get tons of airplay on

MTV, but rap groups that do the same thing get no love? In order for a rap artist to get play on MTV, he has to take his shirt off, bark like a dog, and have a dozen scantily-clad women with Jessica Rabbit proportions gyrating around him like a modern-day harem. I'm convinced that a lot of white people listen to that stuff, in part, because it allows them to confirm what they already think about black men; that our only concerns in life are huge asses, huge diamonds, and huge rims. Fuck MTV.

Chapter 7

When White Rappers Attack

or

Five More Things That Make Me Want to Travel Back in Time and Shoot Kool Herc in the Head

5. Northern State

This white, all-female hip-hop trio from New York enjoyed a brief spurt of media coverage after the release of their sophomore effort. Hopefully, you've never had the misfortune of hearing them. After I read about them in more than one magazine, I stumbled across the CD at a listening station in Virgin Megastore. As I sampled their "music," the effect was similar to the way the aliens in the movie *Mars Attacks* reacted to Slim Whitman songs. A few minutes more and I'm sure that my head would have exploded. Let me be clear on this. Northern State is the worst group in the history of recorded music. Milli and Vanilli scoff at the musical ability, or lack thereof, present in Northern State. (Actually, Milli, née Rob Pilatus, is no longer with us. But if he were, I'm sure he'd be scoffing.) The idea that someone saw fit to give these three a record contract is enough to make me lose all faith in the music industry. Oh, that's right.

That happened *years* ago. The members of Northern State shouldn't even be allowed to set foot in the recording studio, not even to clean up after the band has already left. They are that bad. Here's where white people with balls say, "But Nick. Are they that bad, or do you just dislike them because they're white girls rapping?" And here's where I respond, "No. No. No. They are the most terrible MCs I've ever heard. And I've listened to a lot of hip-hop music. The fact that they're white girls is just the icing on a cake. A horrible, disgusting, non-rapping cake. Oddly enough, they were fortunate enough to work with some incredibly talented people on their second album. ?uestlove—drummer, producer and driving force behind the legendary Roots crew—produced some of the material on the album. If you guys had gotten off your asses and supported all of the amazing music The Roots have produced over the years, he wouldn't have to do shit like this. And isn't there some rule in the music industry that if a girl group is totally devoid of talent that they have to at least be hot pieces of ass? If there isn't, there definitely should be. 50 Cent can't rap worth a damn either, but at least he stays in good shape."

4. Limp Bizkit

Record executive #1: "I have a great idea. Let's combine loud, shitty rock music with loud, shitty pseudo-rapping."

Record executive #2: "Genius. Let's go have lunch."

And thus, the horrible rap-rock hybrid wave of the 90s was released. (Special dispensation to Rage Against The Machine, of course.) The fact that Fred Durst was able to make a living as a recording artist instead of installing carburetors is tempered only by the fact that he's fading so quickly and completely from the consciousness of the average American that many people are probably reading this and thinking, "Fred who?" The success of Limp Bizkit helps to prove one incontrovertible fact of music; if it's loud enough, and aggressive enough, teenage boys will by it. If you don't believe that, see . . .

3. Insane Clown Posse

White guys wearing evil clown makeup doing gangster rap. I wish I were making this up, but they are a real group. People really pay money to listen to two fat white guys in clown makeup rap about whatever it is fat white guys in clown makeup rap about. What would that be exactly? Comparing and contrasting the qualities of different face paints? And what exactly made these clowns insane? I'm certainly not doubting that they are— the fact that they actually go on stage with clown makeup on and try to rap is proof enough that they are, indeed, insane— I'm just curious as to what it was that pushed them over the edge. Whenever I see their albums on the shelves in record stores, I feel like that old Chinese man in the movie *Gremlins*. White people have handled hip-hop the way Zach Galligan handled his mogwai. They simply weren't ready for the responsibility.

2. "Walk This Way"
by Aerosmith & Run D.M.C.

Let me say this up front. Any positive emotions that I feel about this song are completely a result of nostalgia, and nothing more. I was a kid when this was released for Christ's sake. This is a horrible, horrible recording. Run D.M.C. didn't even want to do this damn song. They were talked into doing it by producer Rick Rubin. Far be it for me to bash Rick Rubin. No one appreciates his contribution to the music world more than I do. (Rubin cofounded Def Jam with Russell Simmons in their dorm room at NYU. Now ask yourself what you were doing during your freshman year. Also, while working with the Red Hot Chili Peppers, Rubin discovered some poems that Anthony Kiedis had been working on. On Rubin's suggestion, they put one of them to music. That poem became "Under the Bridge." No Rick Rubin hate here.) A lot of people would say that "Walk This Way" is worthwhile just because it exposed a whole new audience to hip-hop music. Fuck that. If it takes a novelty song for people to become aware of or appreciate an entire genre of music, I'd rather all those people stayed ignorant. Besides, I'd be really skeptical of anyone who claimed to get into hip-hop music as a result of this song. What they probably mean is that they bought one Run D.M.C. album and then went back to listening to The Cure or whatever it was that white people were listening to in 1986.

1. Vanilla Ice

I hate to make the obvious choice, but there's really nothing else that compares. At least Eminem gets the clothes and the attitude right. At least Eminem understood the basic ethos of what a young black American feels because he grew up around it, he lived it. From the beginning, Vanilla Ice seemed like a smug white prick from the suburbs who just wanted to be down when it was convenient to him. I don't think anyone was even remotely surprised when he turned out to be . . . you guessed it: a smug white prick from the suburbs who just wanted to be down. His name was Rob Van Winkle. That tells you all you need to know. The worst part about the success of "Ice Ice Baby" is that it took something that was incredibly cool and ruined it forever. Ice Ice baby is part of a chant that belongs to Alpha Phi Alpha fraternity. Established in 1906 at Cornell University, A Phi A is the oldest of all the black fraternities and sororities and counts among its brotherhood distinguished men like W.E.B. DuBois, Martin Luther King Jr., Thurgood Marshall, Andrew Young, Paul Robeson, and my cousin Steven Jumper. (Did you think a black man was going to get through an entire book without at least one gratuitous shout out? What up, cousin!) But now, whenever they perform at a step show, that cheesy song is always in the back of everyone's mind. Every Alpha alive would be well within his rights to kick Vanilla Ice's monkey ass. (Bonus unintentional comedy alert!) Vanilla Ice once tried to explain how their obvious sample of the Queen/David Bowie classic "Under Pressure" was actually different. Here's what he said, "Theirs goes ding ding ding dingdingdingding. Ding ding ding dingdingdingding. Ours goes ding ding ding dingdingdingding **dingding** ding ding ding ding dingdingdingdin." The scary thing is, I think he was completely serious.

Chapter 8

A Memo to Britney and Justin

Stop referring to black artists as your musical influences. If I have to listen to another of these no-talent, white media creations talk about how much they love Stevie Wonder or how much they're influenced by Michael Jackson, I might just go insane. If you love Stevie Wonder so much, why don't you actually play an instrument on your album? I mean, he was blind and managed to write all his lyrics, compose and arrange his music, play several instruments, sing lead and backup vocals, and produce all the songs. Is it too much to ask of one of these Mickey Mouse Club has-beens to stop shopping for low rise jeans and trucker hats long enough to actually contribute something to their album besides the cover photo? If you're so influenced by Michael Jackson, why don't you stop lip-synching and try singing live? God forbid you should take a second away from your elaborate choreography to worry about the vocals. Also, it is possible to be influenced by someone without totaling ripping off his or her style. I'm looking at you, Justin. His initial solo effort just reeked of MJ. The music. The clothes. The dancing. It was the biggest theft since the Florida elections in 2000. The only thing more annoying than watching a white artist rip off a black artist is watching the media cream their pants over said white artist. I distinctly remember one critic describing Justin Timberlake's solo album as "soulful." Soulful? I have passed gas in my sleep that is more soulful than Justin Timberlake's music. I have heard video game sound effects that are more soulful than Justin Timberlake's music. The sound of my cat coughing up a hairball is more soulful than Justin Timberlake's music. Besides, he doesn't have anything to do with how the music sounds anyway. These pop stars just call whoever the hot producer of the moment is and let them work their magic of creating empty, catch hooks that white people can't resist. What does Justin Timberlake or any of these children know about soul? They've never experienced anything. They've been engulfed in a pop music cocoon since they were preteens. There should be a moratorium on albums recorded by artists who are under 30 years of age. (Obviously, there would be a special Norah Jones exemption.) You wanna be a rock or pop star? Fine. Go live life first. Get your heart broken a few times. Break a few hearts of your own. Drink too much. Maybe develop a drug problem. Spend the night in a county jail somewhere in rural New Mexico. Then, maybe your music won't sound like the jingle to a cereal commercial. It's damn near impossible for a 20-year-old to write, compose, or perform meaningful music; especially if they spend all day being chauffeured around to malls where they perform for children in the food court. "Chick-Fil-A. Are you ready to rock?!"

It's fundamentally wrong for music to be produced this way. For any art of note to be created, the artist must come through some struggle or suffering. Every performer needs to know what it's like to be booed, or worse, ignored. White people took rock & roll from us. White people took hip-hop from us. And now, white people are trying to take R&B from us. The only problem is that none of the white artists have very much rhythm and don't know the first thing about the blues.

Britney. Who would have thought someone with such a white-trash name would ascend to worldwide recognition? I should probably love her. On the surface, she seems like the black man's dream white woman. She's dumb. She's blond. And she's got a big ass. These are all the qualities that we're supposed to love. What more could you ask for? Talent for one thing. She has none. Zero. She can't sing. She doesn't play an instrument. She's a horrible songwriter. I guess she's a decent dancer, but all she does is regurgitate the moves that are taught to her by a chore-ographer. (Which are, of course, mostly re-hashed Michael and Janet Jackson moves.) As a recording artist, Britney Spears is a moderately talented stripper. I would have no problem with her if she were some single mother shaking her ass to pay her way through community college. Instead of paying $17.99 for her album, I'd rather just give her a twenty for a lap dance. I would have no problem with her if she were simply occupying one of the many "hot piece of ass" slots that popular culture reserves for the likes of Carmen Electra or Pamela Anderson. Instead, she's the most successful solo recording artist of this generation. Intelligent, knowledgeable music critics review her albums as if they have any creative merit whatsoever. Her record label spends millions of dollars to market and promote her instead of more deserving artists on its roster. Adults, who should know better, actually purchase her albums. I was in Borders working on this very book and I overheard the conversation of what appeared to be a table full of University of Arizona graduate students. One of the girls had wandered over to the music section and returned with the new Britney CD. It took all my willpower not to turn around and ask her why she bought it. There is absolutely no excuse for that purchase. Unless you own everything that has ever been recorded by Beethoven, Bach, Mozart, Tchaikovsky, Armstrong, Ellington, Coltrane, Davis, The Beatles, The Rolling Stones, The Who, Pink Floyd, Run DMC, Public Enemy, De La Soul, A Tribe Called Quest and anyone else of musical note . . . you should not be buying a Britney Spears CD. It's prepackaged children's music and grown-ups are buying it. Are these same adults eating Lunchables and drinking Capri-Sun too?

There would be more musical merit in an album consisting solely of Keith Richards's snoring. I would rather listen to Bjork blow her nose with no musical accompaniment than listen to Britney Spears's tuneless warbling. But for some reason, America can't get enough of her. Janet Jackson flashes her bejeweled tit on television for less than a second and she's lambasted unmercifully. Britney can appear on *The MTV Video Music Awards* looking like a prostitute with half her ass exposed and white people call her "daring." Amazing. I actually have more respect for prostitutes. For one thing, prostitutes have to actually be good at something. Also, once a prostitute gets paid . . . she goes away. And now, everyone is concerned for her because she appears intent on ruining her All-American girl image that she spent so long crafting. After getting married in Vegas, having it annulled, and then marrying someone who already has a child by another woman, it does seem that she's going a little buck wild. Except for one thing. Behind all the money, makeup and hair extensions, she's just a white-trash girl from Louisiana. This is what they do, people. She's not going crazy. She is fulfilling her destiny.

Chapter 9

A Little Bit Country

veryone loves to make generalizations about minorities. Even minorities like to make generalizations about minorities. Here's one that you can repeat without worrying about anyone taking exception to it. Black people do not like country music. Don't try to tell us that we've just got to listen to so-and-so, or that we should just give it a try. We just do not like it. I know black people who will talk your head off about hip-hop, rock 'n' roll, jazz, acid-jazz, classical, techno, reggae, dub, house, trance, trip-hop, and every other genre that you can think of. But I've never met so much as one person of color who gave a rat's ass about country music. I'm not talking about The Dixie Chicks, Faith Hill, or Shania Twain. That's just Nashville cashing in by giving it a wholesome sheen of tits and ass and then selling it to VH1. Even real country music fans don't like that crap. I'm talking about the down-home stuff. Recently, I noticed a trend in a few albums that I really enjoy. Beck's *Mutations*, Norah Jones's *Feels Like Home* and The Incredible Moses Leroy's *Become the Soft Lightes* all wear their country influences on their sleeves proudly, yet I have no problem enjoying them. What gives? While listening to Ron Fountenberry croon away on "The 4A," I figured it out. It's the voice. Fountenberry—front man for The Incredible Moses Leroy—is a black guy from San Francisco. No southern drawl. When you listen to traditional country music, that twang is unavoidable. Historically, for black people, the deep southern accent that accompanies most country songs meant absolutely nothing but trouble. I'm sure Randy Travis is a hell of a nice guy. Good husband, good father, law-abiding citizen. All that stuff. But thanks to that redneck voice of his, listening to one verse of his song is enough for me to avert my eyes away from any white women in the area and get my butt back over to "my side" of town. After all, these are the same kinds of voices that were heard through the Klan robes. These are the same kinds of voices that were heard from behind the counter at Woolworth's. Even Dolly Parton, who I like as an actress and a personality, can't escape the curse of the twang. She makes a guest appearance on the Norah Jones album and I can never bring myself to finish the entire song. Although in her case, the redneck stigma is the second thing that comes to mind when I hear her voice. Yes. I'm talking about her tremendous breasts. That's how amazing they are. I can hear them when she sings.

It may seem like a stretch, but what other reason can there be? Traditional country is just about one branch away from delta blues on the musical family tree. And the lyrical content of the two genres is remarkably similar. Lots of drinking. Lots of woman/man troubles. The same plaintive, haunting lyrics that make me want to cry when sung by Ted Hawkins would probably make me want to vomit if they were sung by George Strait. I know there are some black people who find the deep south accent charming or quaint. These are the people who spent the weekend in Chapel Hill when they dropped their daughter off for her freshman year at UNC. These are the people who had to spend a week in Birmingham for work. They didn't live there. They never had to stop for gas outside of Sumter, South Carolina, and see their mother disrespected by the buck-toothed high school dropout working behind the counter. They never walked into a Cracker Barrel restaurant in Little Rock, Arizona, and watched every head in the place turn and follow them until they sat down. They never saw the looks of incredulity on the faces of their lifelong schoolmates when they discovered that you were going to a much better university than they were. All those people sounded like the hicks in the country music songs. I don't want to hear anything those people have to say. Yes. I know I'm stereotyping an entire genre of music and a huge segment of the white population, but fuck it. There are millions of white Americans who dismiss all hip-hop music as incoherent garbage just because of the way 50 Cent sounds. So, I say turnabout is fair play.

Just in case anyone feels any ambiguity in this essay, I'll go ahead and make my point Crystal Gayle clear. Country music sucks.

Chapter 10

Except . . .

. . . For Charlie Pride. That nigger is a genius. Or a fool. I'm not exactly sure which one. But he's the only black guy in country music, so I have to give him some love. This Bud's for you Charlie.

Chapter 11

Party Time

I mentioned earlier that if we're going to live together, we have to socialize together. If you hang out with us enough, eventually you're going to find yourself in a party situation. Maybe you've had a few drinks and the urge to shake your groove thing is just too strong to resist. Fine. Go for it. But do so with these words of wisdom in mind.

White women, don't go out of your way to show us what a great dancer you are. Chances are, you aren't very good and you'll just end up making a fool out of yourself. Every weekend, in night clubs all across the country, some white woman walks into the joint and heads straight to the dance floor as if she's the love child of John Travolta and Paula Abdul, only to reveal that she's actually the unholy dancing devil spawn of Mark Madsen and Elaine Benes. Does that mean that all white women should just avoid the dance floor altogether? Of course not. If you wanna dance, dance. But there's no need to make an undue spectacle of yourself by waving your arms around in the air and screaming "whoo hoo" at the top of your lungs. (In general, white women, you shouldn't even be screaming "whoo hoo" once you've left college. I think "whoo hoo" is derived from a Sanskrit word that means "I'm a drunken idiot.")

If you guys are so concerned with black people making fun of the way you dance, why do you keep giving us so much ammunition? At every night club in American there is one white woman who thinks that she's hot shit because all the black guys are checking her out. What she doesn't realize is that they are only staring at her because she's doing the running man to a Sade song. (Which, when you think about it, is just as impressive as it is embarrassing.) It's a vicious cycle. Crazy dancing causes stares. Stares breed false confidence. False confidence breeds more crazy dancing.

The amazing thing about these "spectacle dancers" is that, for the most part, black people don't dance like that. Sure, there are always a handful of young bucks at the club who are trying to live out their *Soul Train* fantasies. But your average twenty-something, thirty-something club/partygoer is just trying to have some fun, not get a full blown cardiovascular workout. I can stay on the dance floor for hours at a time and never pick my feet up off the ground. Call it the low-impact boogie. By utilizing a complex system of hand gestures, facial expressions, pelvic thrusts, head bobs, and buttock gyrations, I can express more soul and emotion than an entire troupe of 18-year-old break dancers in full performance mode.

If a white person insists on attempting the more exotic dances, they should be undertaken with extreme caution. If the move is too new, people will think you are just some weird white person doing a weird white person dance. If the move is too old, people will think you are just some lame white person who is painfully behind the times. Even if your cultural timing is just right, it would probably come off as if you're just trying too hard to fit in. It's like the uneducated person who learns a big word and goes out of his way to use it in conversation, no matter if it is appropriate or not. In fact, you should just forget the more elaborate dances altogether. I would advise finding one or two versatile moves that you really like and sticking with those from here on out. I've been doing the same dances since my junior year of college and I can say the same for just about every halfway decent dancer I know. (I do the Nick dance, my wife does the Tasha dance, etc.)

I address this particular tip to white women specifically because white men don't seem to have this problem. If you get a white guy out on the dance floor, he's got enough common sense to keep it as low-key as he possibly can. He knows that he is in the cultural cross hairs and he doesn't want to bring too much attention to himself. The next time you go to a wedding, check out the white guy. First, he doesn't even get out on the floor until everyone is sufficiently drunk and he knows no one will notice him. Then, when he does hit the floor, he keeps it simple. They all do the same exact dance. White man overbite, thumbs out, step from side to side. Repeat until your significant other is ready to sit down. When you are observing these guys, please do them a favor and try not to distract them. Usually their attention will be focused on their own feet, for fear of losing the beat. If you should happen to catch their gaze, smile politely and go back to scamming on that one attractive bridesmaid or groomsman. These kinds of dancers must have complete and total concentration. The last thing they need is you throwing them off. Nodding at them, waving at them, or just giving them the thumbs up during the closing seconds of "Celebration" could be disastrous. They might be forced to spend the duration of "YMCA" finding the rhythm again.

There are also the white guys who just err on the side of caution and do not dance. Ever. Sure, the wives and girlfriends of these guys are probably more than a bit rhythmically frustrated, but I respect these gentlemen immensely. These are the men who realize that they are horrible dancers and have chosen to avoid the embarrassment. You have to appreciate the level of pride inherent in that choice. It takes a big person to admit that they are just no good at something and avoid doing it altogether. After this past Christmas, I made a promise to myself. I'm never wrapping another gift again. Ever. I'm horrible at it. Whatever combination of skill sets that is required to complete this particular task—hand eye coordination, depth perception, opposable thumbs—I just do not have. I'm so bad that whenever I wrap a gift to send to a member of my family, I envision them opening it and going, "Awww. They must have had some retarded kids doing gift wrapping at the mall this year." I'm not good at it, and I'm not doing it anymore. (But gift wrapping does require using both scissors and tape; two things that I have a long, sad history of being inept with. My mother loved to tell the story of my kindergarten report card. Reading: excellent. Writing: excellent. Math: excellent. Arts & Crafts: unsatisfactory.) If Jennifer Lopez could make that same admission we'd all be spared her horrible, horrible albums. But then we wouldn't have any reason to see her shake her ass would we? Hmmm. Interesting conundrum. There needs to be some sort of pop culture think tank to tackle issues like this. I'm not suggesting that we put the country's best and brightest minds to work on this though. What I have in mind is a group of moderately intelligent, state-school-educated men and women who put their slightly higher-than-average brain power to use for good and not evil. As for Jennifer, if she doesn't start picking better movie roles, the heterosexual men and homosexual women of the world might not be seeing her nearly as much anyway. *Maid in Manhattan*? What sense does that make?

"Jennifer, you're a Puerto Rican girl from the Bronx who has busted her ample ass and made a big splash in the world of show business. You command huge sums of money for roles, and you are one of only a handful of bona fide female box office draws. You can have your pick of the best parts. You can get a big budget movie the green light. You could also choose to champion a smaller movie that might not get made otherwise and help it see the light of day. What do you want to do next?"

"I want to play a Puerto Rican maid!"

What? Why not just make it a Disney remake and call it *Spicarella* while you're at it?

But back to the dancing. I'm not sure if white people realize this, but you don't *have* to do what the song tells you to do. When House of Pain tells you to "Jump Around," or Kris Kross tells you to "Jump," it's really more of a suggestion than it is a demand. If you feel like you must comply, then feel free to do it once or twice during the song, but three and a half minutes of jumping up and down isn't fun to anyone but Richard Simmons and a few hyperactive four-year-olds. Just relax, and do your own thing. Given the explicit state of some of the lyrics to today's songs, you really should just get into the habit of ignoring what they're saying altogether anyway. For women, exhibiting the behavior suggested in most music that's played at clubs these days would probably get you arrested, raped, or both. At the very least, you'd end up being totally confused.

At one point, while working as a writer's assistant on a talk show at BET, our musical guest was Nelly. When he sang the lyric, "Andale, andale mommy e-I-e-I uh ooooh," I turned to one of the writers and said, "Lyrics officially do not matter any-more." So, you don't have to jump. And you definitely do not have to throw your hands in the air, or wave them like you just don't care. Even if you don't care, I do. And I'm not interested in having your hands in my face while I'm trying to enjoy a night out with my bitch . . . I mean my wife. (What did I tell you? That's the effect that rap music can have on you.) Obviously, you should feel free to wave your hands in the air if you're at a concert or something, but everyone is high then anyway and no one will care.

The non-jumping suggestion gets more and more relevant as you get older. The last thing anyone wants to see on their Saturday night out is some white guy pulling a hamstring or spraining an ankle because he was attempting some overly ath-letic dance moves while wearing Birkenstocks. If you're simply overwhelmed by your desire to "Jump," might I suggest the very popular faux jump? That's when you bend at the knees and bob your head up and down. Kind of like jumping up and down without your feet ever actually leaving the ground. You burn al-most as many calories, and it's a lot easier on your joints. It's like the dance equivalent of power walking instead of jogging.

I should point out that there is a reason for my extreme loathing of instructional dance songs. I'm a lot more fiercely in-dependent than most when it comes to dancing. To me, danc-ing is a very personal form of expression. That's why I totally reject the concept of line dancing. If the Electric Slide breaks out, then I break out. (Break out is Negro vernacular for leaving. I probably should have just included a glossary, huh?) What could possibly be less fun than doing the exact same dance as all of the other one hundred people on the dance floor? Perhaps after we do the Electric Slide we can all join in and do the root canal shuffle, and then maybe a few minutes of the prostate exam hop? I'm sure there would be plenty of volunteers to teach Ms. Lopez how to do the latter. Be warned white Americans. If you guys don't take my advice, I'm going to be forced to capitalize on your good nature. I'll have to record an album consisting only of instructional party anthems and put you to good use. I can see me burning up the charts with songs like, "Vote Sharpton," "Reparations, Now," and "Credit Approval (Is All I Need)."

Most of the things that I've mentioned so far in this book have been fairly lighthearted. I assure you that what I am about to write is not intended to be tongue in cheek. Heeding this next bit of advice could save you from serious bodily injury some day. I call it the Adams theory of dance floors. It is as follows: The space that you are allowed to occupy on a dance floor is inversely proportional to the number of people who are on said dance floor. Adjust accordingly. I know, I know. It sounds incredibly simple. But if we are all going to party together, white people must grasp this concept. (There is also the Adams theory of car stereos. That one states that someone's taste in music is inversely proportional to the power of his car stereo.) If the dance floor is relatively empty, feel free to go nuts. You can thrash and gyrate to your heart's content. Gesticulate with your arms. Whip your hair this way and that. But once the crowd thickens, you have to restrict your movements. It's common courtesy and common sense. I can't tell you how many times I've been tripping the light fantastic with my squeeze, only to be rudely awakened from my disco reverie by the brutal slap of long blond hair in my face. Nothing is worse than watching your significant other be violently shoved from behind over and over by an oblivious white couple's exaggerated swaying. What is it about dance floors that elicit this ridiculous behavior from white people? Would you haphazardly change lanes back and forth on the interstate in rush hour traffic? If you were on an airplane, would you put your feet in the lap of the person to your left and your head in the lap of the person to your right and go to sleep? If you were in a restaurant, would you reach over and sample a total stranger's entrée? Of course you wouldn't. But for some reason, white people feel like it's OK to totally infringe on others' personal space in their futile search for the two and the four. Many people reading this book—mostly white—are probably thinking that this is a grossly inaccurate generalization. It's not. I'm not saying that *all* white people do this. I'm saying that *no* black people do. We just know better. Maybe it's instinctive. Maybe we learned it through all the years during which any unnecessary contact with someone other than your dance partner could set off a huge brawl, ending everyone's party for the night. I'm not sure how we acquired this knowledge, but it's there. If you doubt me, I invite you to conduct a little pop sociological experiment.

I want you to go to a night club in the blackest part of your town. The smaller and more ghetto the place, the better. Find a good seat, and wait. Wait until the dance floor is absolutely packed. Wait until it's so full that you're thinking about calling the fire marshal. Wait until you find yourself thinking that not one more person could possible set foot on the dance floor, then wait until ten more people join in the fun. Once the dance floor reaches that maximum density, watch. Just observe. Do you know what you'll see in that teeming, writhing mass of hormonally charged black and brown bodies? Cooperation. Uniform, unspoken cooperation. Each individual understanding that his personal dance area is getting smaller and smaller and making the proper adjustments until everyone on the floor is basically standing still and rocking side to side and front to back ever so slightly with their arms close to their bodies. Big strong men rubbing butts with other big strong men. The sweat from one woman's back co-mingling with the sweat from another woman's back. Couples whose rhythms have become syncopated so that Jack & Jill's rocking and swaying doesn't interfere with Dick & Jane's moving and grooving. Fucking beautiful.

For my first full-time job after college, I worked as desk assistant for NBC News in Washington, D.C. It's the starting point for a job in network news, and it was an incredible experience. (During my time there, I was on the receiving end of a memorable, expletive-laced tirade from the aforementioned Mr. Brokaw. Did I mention he was a jackass?) All of the desk assistants were in their early twenties, and from time to time we all went out as a group and enjoyed the night life of our nation's capital. I began to notice that whenever it came time to select a place for our next outing, the establishments were always conspicuously devoid of minorities. Now, if anyone is used to partying with white people, it's me. But it just seemed odd that someone would live in one of the blackest cities in America, yet want to totally steer clear of socializing with red, yellow, brown or black people. Whenever I suggested going someplace where the crowd was a little more diverse, I was met with startling apathy.

Allow me to explain something. Just going to a predominantly black club does not guarantee that you're going to get your ass kicked. I think some white Americans envision walking into a club, hearing the record scratch to a sudden halt, and then hearing someone shout, "White people. Get 'em!" There really is nothing for you to be afraid of. As long as you act like you've got some sense, you're no more likely to be harassed than I am. Sure, you might be a little uncomfortable at first. But how much fun would life be if you never left your comfort zone? Besides, most black people have to leave their comfort zone every time they go to work. Whenever I go into a bar, restaurant, or night club that is patronized by a mostly white crowd, I still perform what I like to think of as the emergency black check. Basically, what I'm doing is surveying the area for any other black men who might be able to watch my back in the event of some unforeseen situation. Not that I don't trust white people. But you never know. Just knowing that there's a brother over by the jukebox and another one at the end of the bar allows me to enjoy myself a lot more. It's similar to the demonstration that flight attendants give to point out the emergency exits once you're seated on an airplane. Now, for my own safety, I know that there are Negroes conveniently located to the front, sides, and rear of the establishment.

Partying with black folks is a lot safer than it used to be. During the first Gangster Rap era—right before the Mesozoic, just after the Paleolithic—there were a lot more dangers to watch out for. During the late 1980s and early 1990s black men from all over the country had been inundated with tales of Crips & Bloods, Uzis and nine millimeters, and blasting back at police officers. Never mind the fact there were no Crips or Bloods within five hundred miles of most places in this country, there were always plenty of brothers who were willing to fight at the drop of a hat. Literally.

"Fool. You knocked my hat off!"

"My fault, bruh. Sorry about that."

"Sorry? Sorry don't give me back my respect, bitch."

Seriously. It was that bad at times. Imagine being a teenage male in a party or club. You are simultaneously trying to: ogle every breast, thigh, and butt in the place, keep one eye on your watch so that you don't get home too late, and maintain the aura of detached cool for which teenage males are known. On top of all that, you have to make sure that you don't step on anyone's new Nikes, don't bump into anyone, don't look at anyone's girlfriend, and oh yeah . . . try and have a good time. Thank God those days are long gone.

The phenomenon that leaves white people expecting us to feel comfortable with them without them reciprocating has been around since integration. I remember having a conversation with someone in college about our school cafeteria.

"Nick, why do the black people always sit on the right side of the pit?"

"Why do white people always sit on the left side?"

"Ummm . . . good point."

Here is the problem. White people always expect us to make the overtures. We're always expected to put ourselves out there and take the risks. Maybe the thinking is, "We brought them all the way over here from Africa, the least they could do is go out for drinks with us after work." If we're going to ever truly understand each other, both sides have to take some risks. God knows I've taken my fair share. Some of them turned out better than others, but I'm still glad I made the attempt.

March, 1995: Tried karaoke for the first and last time.

October, 1997: Tasted turnips. So that's how white people stay thin.

June, 2001: Went to a techno club. All the ecstasy in the world wouldn't be enough for me to stomach that godforsaken music.

August, 2004: Snorkeling. Loved it. Blacks and Hispanics have this strange belief that, if you enter the ocean, you'll immediately drown or be attacked by a huge great white shark. I think white people made movies like *Jaws* just so they could keep the beach all to themselves.

So, put this book down right now. Wait, finish this paragraph first. Then, put this book down, and go out to a club that is mostly black. Relax, follow my rules, and have fun.

Chapter 12

Burn, Hollywood, Burn

he next time someone tells you about how far black actors and actresses have come, punch them in the stomach. Or, if you're not in the mood to risk a possible ass-kicking or civil litigation, tell them to watch *Monster's Ball*. I thought Halle Berry was incredible in the role, and I think that she deserved the Academy Award for it. I just couldn't help but be amazed by how much more she had to do than her white counterparts. Julia Roberts received the Oscar for *Erin Brockovich*. All that role required of her was to put on a push-up bra and a pair of high-heeled Candies and sashay around the San Fernando Valley with her signature blend of spunk and wit that America has come to know and love. Let's be honest here. Any decent actress could have done that in her sleep. They were just waiting to give Julia an Oscar. Meanwhile, Halle Berry had to get sodomized by *Sling Blade* himself. I am, of course, referring to the now-legendary sex scene between Ms. Berry and Mr. Billy Bob Thornton. Is that what it takes for a black actress to get nominated? If that's the case, then the Academy of Motion Picture Arts and Sciences owes several dozen retroactive Oscars to Jeannie Pepper, Heather Hunter, and Ebony Ayes. These legendary African-American porn stars have been ravaged by a combined number of approximately 750 white actors in a combined 250 movies. Surely there is at least one Oscar-worthy performance in that bunch somewhere. (If I had a vote, I would give the nod to Ms. Hunter for her performance in *Screw the Right Thing*. It brought tears to my eyes.) If you haven't seen *Monster's Ball*, I'll give you the theme of the movie: Hot chicks cure racism. That's it in a nutshell. Billy Bob's character is a mean, racist son of a bitch. He threatens some young black boys for coming onto his property. He calls one of his fellow prison guards a nigger. Then, he meets Halle Berry and—poof!—racism gone. Just like that. Next thing you know, Halle Berry is bent over on the couch and Billy Bob is pounding away. Near the end of the movie he says to her, "I just want to take care of you." No shit, Billy Bob. She's Halle Berry! Every heterosexual man and homosexual woman in the world wants to "take care" of Halle Berry. Hell, there are probably a few homosexual men and heterosexual women who want to "take care" of Halle Berry. You want to prove to me that you're not a racist? Why don't you shack up with Star Jones for a while? Go a few rounds on that couch with Whoopie Goldberg just so we can make sure you don't have any of those old prejudices left.

Giving Halle Berry the Oscar was a safe choice for Hollywood. Because of her biracial heritage, Halle has the lighter skin complexion and delicate features that are closer to the white American standard of beauty. She made a name for herself playing eye candy parts in movies like *Strictly Business*, *The Flintstones*, *B.A.P.S.*, and *Bullworth* before breaking out of the typecasting shell and receiving universal acclaim in the HBO movie *Introducing Dorothy Dandridge*. Oddly enough, she gave us a glimpse of the kind of performance that she was capable of in one of her very first roles as Samuel L. Jackson's crackhead girlfriend in Spike Lee's *Jungle Fever*. To this day, there are people who refuse to believe me when I tell them that was Halle Berry. Her character in *Monster's Ball* was poor, uneducated, married to a man on death row, and not a particularly good mother to her son. It wasn't threatening to the image that Hollywood has always been comfortable seeing black women in. Although I'm sure it was challenging for her as an actress, it wasn't particularly uplifting for women or minorities. Not that those qualities should be a requirement for black actresses when selecting roles, or for the Academy when selecting Oscar-worthiness, but she was basically doing the same thing Hattie McDaniels did fifty years ago minus about seventy pounds and the head scarf. At any point I was expecting her to tell Billy Bob Thornton that she didn't know nothin' 'bout birthing no babies. I could be reading way too much into this, but I can't help but believe that playing this kind of role was a factor. You only need to go back a few years to Angela Basset's portrayal of Tina Turner in *What's Love Got to Do with It* to see an actress of color give an incredible performance in a role that was almost the exact opposite of *Monster's Ball*. Playing a confident, kick-ass black woman who refuses to accept horrible treatment from her incredibly talented husband doesn't get you an Oscar, but playing a put-upon, ignorant, black woman who accepts solace in the arms of a racist does? What a wacky town.

I can't help but notice a similar dichotomy in the career of Denzel Washington. In *Malcolm X*, he gave the performance of a lifetime. We're talking Robert DeNiro in *Raging Bull*, Al Pacino in *The Godfather II*, or Eddie Murphy in *Trading Places*. (I'm dead serious.) He was that good. Even though he doesn't look anything like Malcolm X, you forget that you're watching a fictional account of the man's life and almost feel as if you're watching a documentary consisting of actual footage. It was the kind of part that actors spend their entire careers waiting for and, when he got his chance, he knocked it out of the park. He was nominated for, but didn't receive the Best Actor Oscar. (Pacino won for *Scent of a Woman*. People are still talking about his performance in that movie, but not in the same way that they talk about Denzel's. Granted, Washington won a Best Supporting actor Oscar in 1989, but Best Actor is a significant step up in respect and clout.) Then, he took a schmaltzy, melodramatic movie like *The Hurricane* and turned it into a one-man tear jerker. Witness the power of Denzel. At some point during the movie, Rueben Carter speaks these lines from behind bars, "Hate put me in here, but love's gonna bust me out." Ouch. That's the kind of dialogue that a good screen writer writes and then immediately deletes while shaking his head. My fingers almost refused to allow me to type those words. When I saw that line in the trailer, I actually winced audibly and made the same face that Lee Harvey Oswald made when Jack Ruby shot him in the stomach in that parking garage in Dallas. Amazingly, when the scene rolls around in the movie, Denzel makes it work. No Oscar there either. Then comes *Training Day*. Not a horrible movie, but not a great movie by any stretch. Ethan Hawke gives his usual slack jawed, dumbfounded performance—he and Keanu Reeves pioneered that school of acting of which Toby McGuire and Elijah Wood are ardent followers—which is thankfully offset by a brief but spectacular appearance by a semi-nude Eva Mendes. So what are we left with? Denzel having fun playing a crooked cop. It was his version of Al Pacino in *The Devil's Advocate*. A great actor having fun with a role in a sub-par movie. And he wins an Oscar.

Two great performances of strong black men who were persecuted by white Americans but never lost their dignity or pride. Two strong black men who realized their shortcomings as men and addressed them head-on under the most difficult circumstances you could imagine. Two strong black men who had all the reasons in the world to hate white Americans across the board until the end of time, but instead chose to embrace society as a whole to foster change. Those performances weren't worthy. But a crooked, drug abusing, philandering, thieving, scheming, ego-maniacal cop . . . that gets the Academy Award? I know this is where I'll lose a lot of white readers, but you've come this far so maybe you'll humor me. I refuse to believe that is a coincidence. I know the Academy gives make-up Oscars all the time. They did it for Pacino with *Scent of a Woman*. They did it for Paul Newman with *The Color of Money*. But when they only give the Academy Award for best actor to a black person once every twenty years or so, they should really try and make it count. I'm convinced that Denzel Washington was almost offended by it. I remember watching the awards that night, looking at his face, and thinking, "He's pissed." Go back and look at the footage. He did not look happy. He didn't look relieved. He didn't look vindicated. He looked insulted. And he should have been. It allows the narrow-minded idiots out there to believe that Hollywood is somehow practicing some sort of Academy Award affirmative action. They can look down their noses at Denzel Washington when they've never even seen his best work. Then, of course, he had to go backstage and answer a litany of questions about being a black actor and winning the award instead of questions about being an actor and winning the award. I'm sure Denzel felt proud for his people, but winning the Oscar should be about acting. Period. That's the time when actors should be answering questions about craft, preparation, and character study. He didn't win the Blackademy award. He has never been a guest on Inside the Blacktor's Studio. He's just a fucking actor.

I don't think that white people understand that, on some level, to keep referring to him as a black actor is insulting. It's as if this allows him to be kept in some category that is separate from Tom Hanks and Russell Crowe. Oh yeah. At this point, I could very easily launch into a tirade against two of the worst Best Supporting winners in recent memory. Cuba Gooding Jr. winning for *Jerry McGuire*, and Martin Landau of *Ed Wood* beating out Samuel L. Jackson for *Pulp Fiction*. But if I did, I would end up striking down upon thee with great vengeance and furious anger, those who attempt to poison and destroy my brothers. And you will know I am the Lord when I lay my vengeance upon thee. Right now, the *Pulp Fiction* fans are probably smiling from ear to ear, but the rest of you are thinking that I've lost my mind.

The racial double standard even applies to white people in Hollywood. Stephen Spielberg is one of the movie industry's true golden boys. And for good reason. No other director in history has combined critical and box office success like he has. Almost every critic's or moviegoer's all time top ten list contains at least one Spielberg film. There was no such thing as a summer blockbuster before *Jaws*. You would think that someone of his stature would get the benefit of the doubt when dealing with issues of race on film. You would be wrong. Allow me to explain. Spielberg has directed three historical films. *Schindler's List*, about a concentration camp, received universal acclaim. *Saving Private Ryan*, a WWII drama, received universal acclaim. *Amistad,* which dealt with issues of slavery here in the United States, was met with mixed reviews.

OK, maybe it's just a coincidence. Maybe it's a coincidence that the one movie of the three that didn't show America in a positive light wasn't embraced. Maybe it's a coincidence that people had no problem dealing with the horrors of a concentration camp in Nazi Germany and no problem dealing with the horrors of combat in WWII, but the horrors of the Middle Passage were just too much to take. Maybe it's a coincidence that the movie-going public has gotten down on their knees and fellated almost every other movie that Stephen Spielberg has given them, but just didn't appreciate this film. To quote Samuel L. Jackson from *Pulp Fiction* again, "I'd like to believe that, but that shit ain't the truth." The truth is that Americans didn't want to see that stuff. You can talk about all the stuff the Nazis did; just don't air any of our dirty laundry. We still can't handle it. We didn't want to see it.

I remember sitting in a mostly empty movie theater in Santa Monica the weekend the movie opened thinking, "This is a Spielberg film. Where is everybody?" After reviews and box office numbers began coming in, I began to wonder if maybe good old Steve had just misfired. But I couldn't help but remember the woman who was sitting near me crying her eyes out when Djimon Hounsou tore his clothes off in front of that bonfire and shouted, "Give us free! Give us free!" I double-dog dare you to find a more gripping, emotionally wrenching moment in the history of cinema. He did everything you could have asked for with that subject matter. And America just didn't want to see it.

But why focus on the negative aspects of race in Hollywood? After all, blacks are now writing, directing, and producing their own films. Surely, that's a good thing. I guess so. But it also gives way to what my wife and I refer to as the anti-stereotype stereotype. This is the kind of movie in which a well-meaning black writer or director attempts to counteract years of negative images in one movie. The best example of this is Malcolm D. Lee's 1999 film, *The Best Man*. The movie centers around a group of young, black, twenty-something college classmates who are all reuniting for a wedding. The main character, played by Taye Diggs, is a novelist whose most recent book contains thinly veiled versions of all his former classmates. Skeletons are unearthed and many scandalous secrets are revealed. It's not a bad premise for a movie at all. It's the execution that leaves a lot to be desired. In his rush to provide positive images, Lee instead creates unbelievable, one-dimensional characters.

The group consists of Diggs's writer character, whose novel is all set to be published. Nia Long's character appears to be an executive producer at *BET News*, even though she's clearly in her mid to late twenties. Morris Chestnut's character is an all-pro running back for the New York Giants. Harold Perrineau Jr.'s character is doing the noble schoolteacher thing by working in a school in a rough neighborhood in Harlem. And even though Terrence Howard's character is supposed to be unemployed and somewhat down on his luck, he's an amazing guitar player who makes regular appearances in a night club.

Where are the people who are in graduate school just because they wanted to put off having to enter the workforce? Where are the investment bankers who hate their jobs and are contemplating a total career change, but don't want to give up making really good money? Where are the elementary school teachers who love the work, but don't know if they can take being underpaid and underappreciated for their entire professional career? Where are the real people? Surely, there have to be movies by and about black people that manage to avoid falling into the trap of stereotyped buffoonery, but also don't give in to the urge to paint a totally idyllic picture of anyone with dark skin?

After Spike Lee burst onto the scene with *She's Gotta Have It*, and then *Do The Right Thing*, people began to predict—which made black people expect—this wave of young, talented black filmmakers to come forth doing increasingly more artistic and distinctive movies. Those directors never really came. The few young guns who did seem poised to pick up the torch and run—the Hughes brothers, John Singleton—seemed to falter under the pressure of being labeled the "next great black director." There have been several attempts at more independent-style filmmaking. The problem is that we don't support those films. Movies like *Love Jones*, *Eve's Bayou*, and *Crazy as Hell* were honest, respectable attempts at filmmaking. None of the characters were rapping, selling drugs, or playing basketball. The directors also weren't trying to save the world or uplift the race. They were just trying to tell interesting stories about interesting characters. And no one saw those movies.

White people didn't go see them because they generally don't go to see movies about black people. And black people didn't go see them because, for the most part, they didn't even know about them. Why is that? Because white people don't promote the movies that they don't think black people will go see. It's a chicken vs. the egg argument and I don't know who is more to blame, the white executives or the black movie patrons, but I do know that *Barbershop* made twice as much money as *The Antwone Fisher Story*, and there is something fundamentally wrong with that. Perhaps if Denzel Washington had cast a rapper to play the lead role in his directorial debut instead of the talented, previously unknown Derek Luke? Sure, Busta Rhymes wouldn't have been able to give the same nuanced, emotionally vulnerable performance, but the soundtrack would have been off the hook!

I take my hat off to Samuel L. Jackson for calling Hollywood out on this idiotic practice of hiring rappers instead of actual actors. In a *Sacramento Bee* article, Jackson is quoted as saying, "To take people from the music world and give them the same kind of credibility and weight that you give me, Morgan Freeman, Laurence Fishburne, Forest Whitaker—that's like an aberration to me. It's not my job to lend credibility to so-and-so rapper who's just coming into the business." And he's right. First of all, most of them suck. (I'm making a special Mos Def/Queen Latifah exception. Those two are very gifted actors as well as just amazing all-around performers. So much so that I'm willing to give Latifah a pass on *Bringing Down the House*. And *Beauty Shop*. And *Taxi*. On second thought, fuck that. No pass for Latifah.)

Ice Cube, LL Cool J, Busta Rhymes, DMX; they're all just terrible actors. And it's not like they're being asked to play Hamlet. These guys are basically cast to play some sort of version of themselves, and they can't even manage to do that. Secondly, I refuse to believe that just casting a rapper in a secondary role in a movie like *S.W.A.T.* or *Shaft* actually brings an audience to the movie. I doubt that the fact that Ludacris is in *2 Fast, 2 Furious* is going to be the deciding factor on your spending your $8.50. If it is, you're either the world's biggest Ludacris fan or an absolute idiot. (In either case, you're probably not reading this book so why am I even talking about you any more?) Lastly, it takes work away from people who need and deserve it.

Every time a director casts a rapper in even a bit part in a major Hollywood film, that's an opportunity that could have served as the breakthrough for some struggling actor or actress. For the hip-hop star turned actor, these parts are just something to do in between albums or concert tours. For an actor who has yet to make a name for himself, these parts could be the launching point for an entire career. At the very least, it would allow them to quit their day job and pay their bills through acting, a feat that the vast majority of the thousands of actors living in Los Angeles and New York never accomplish. Imagine Francis Ford Coppola deciding who's going to play the character Clean in *Apocalypse Now*. What if instead of casting a young Laurence Fishburne, he had decided to go with Tito Jackson because he was more recognizable? Go ahead and laugh. Then try to picture Tito's afro riding down the river with Martin Sheen and totally ruining that movie. Not so funny now is it?

I say turnabout is fair play. If we're going to keep letting rappers give bad performances in movies, why not start letting some actors record some bad rap albums. I'll bet that Louis Gossett Jr. has some skills on the microphone. Of course we'd have to give him a wardrobe overhaul and a stage name. I think that people would pay to hear an album full of dope rhymes from my main man LG2.

But back to black movies. Whenever black people complain about the coonishness—another new word—of the latest Wayans brothers' movie, there is someone there to defend it. Their protest usually goes something like this, "But there are silly comedies for white people. Why can't we have them?" The problem is that white America gets to go to the movies on Friday night with a choice. Do I go watch a mature, intelligent film with gifted and hardworking actors? Or do I turn off my brain for an hour and a half and laugh at fart jokes? Black America doesn't get to make that decision. For the most part, the former does not exist for us. And if it does, it gets no budget, no marketing and it's out of theaters within a few weeks. The latter is shoved down your throat beginning sixth months before it opens and ends up seeping its way into our national subconscious and then a bunch of people end up seeing *Soul Plane* almost as an afterthought. For every Farrelly brothers there is a Wes Anderson. For every Adam Sandler movie, there is another Christopher Guest mockumentary. For every Tara Reid, there is a Scarlett Johansson. White people get to make comedies about eccentric genius families and companies that can erase your memories. Black people get to make comedies about barbershops and cookouts. That's not exactly a recipe for great cinema. If you get too far out of the creative black box, Hollywood shoves you back in line or pushes you out of the way altogether.

The small screen does not escape my wrath. I grew up watching tons of television. When I look back at the shows that I watched as a child, I'm amazed at how much racism there was on television. Two of my favorite cartoons were *The Flintstones* and *The Jetsons*. According to those shows, there were no black people in the past and there weren't going to be any black people in the future. Sure, in the future we'll have robot maids and talking dogs, but black people will have long since gone the way of the dinosaur. Seriously, how racist is that? Some futuristic cartoon white person hated black people so much that he didn't even want them in his home long enough to clean up the place. So, he goes out and invents a robot that can do it. I bet they managed to keep at least a few dozen black people around just to keep the NBA at least a little entertaining.

Welcome Back Kotter. Racist. The show focused on a group of underachieving ethnic students called the Sweathogs. Nice way to send a positive message to the kids, guys. The Sweathogs consisted of a Puerto Rican thug, a Jewish nerd, an Italian dufus, and a poor dumb black Sweathog who only opened his mouth once an episode to say, "Hi there." Up your nose with a rubber hose ABC for putting that show on the air. Although I must say, best theme song ever. (And this is the best segue ever.) Even the theme songs for some shows managed to offend. Sounds impossible doesn't it? Think about it. *Happy Days* was probably the whitest show of all time. What were they singing in their theme song? "Sunday, Monday . . . Happy Days. Tuesday, Wednesday . . . Happy Days." We had no idea white people had this much fun all week long.

Let's ride over to the south side of TV town to a black show like *The Jeffersons*. What are they singing about? "Grits don't burn in the kitchen. Beans don't burn on the grill." What the fuck? Beans on the grill? George Jefferson was supposed to be a successful entrepreneur. He had a deluxe apartment on the East side after all. But according to the people who wrote the theme song he wasn't smart enough to figure out that you couldn't cook beans on the grill. I cut my man Norman Lear some slack because of his overall body of work and the fact that he let a black man call a white man "honky" once a week on the show.

Even when shows were created by black people, there was still a hint of negativity. One of my favorite shows of all time was *Fat Albert and the Cosby Kids*. The show initially caught my eye because it was a cartoon about black people—something I had never seen before. Up until that point, I wasn't sure if we could even be animated. Maybe we didn't stand still long enough for the artists to get a look at us? Maybe there wasn't enough brown ink at Hanna-Barbera? Who knows? Of course the show was created by Bill Cosby. We all know that Cos tries to keep it positive, so in every episode there was a moral or a bit of advice for the kids. One episode might tell us to stay in school. Another might tell us to leave the drugs alone. I remember coming up with my own positive message. Hey kids. Don't play in the city dump. Yeah. Kids don't make musical instruments out of other people's garbage and put your mouths on them.

Fat Albert and the gang hung out in the dump. Is that Cos's idea of a good example for the kids? And how about another one for the kids? Don't steal. If you remember, they had a television set in their clubhouse that they used to watch *The Brown Hornet*. Where did that come from? Were we supposed to believe that a black family in South Philly just had an extra color television lying around their house that one of the kids brought in? I don't care what kind of household you grew up in. White, black, yellow, red or brown. Lower class, middle class or upper class. There is no such thing as an *extra* television set. It does not exist. If you can put a TV in the living room and every bedroom and still have one left over, then you put it in the kitchen. If you have the kitchen covered, next comes the master bathroom. Hell, I'd stack one television on top of another television before I'd just give one away. They stole that TV. The only other option is that they somehow found a television in the dump and were able to repair it. Right. I just don't see a guy named *Dumb* Donald or a guy named *Weird* Harold being an electronics whiz. But I suspected Fat Albert was a thief anyway.

The old cartoons were a lot more primitive than the ones kids watch today. The background animation wasn't nearly as detailed. So, when Albert was walking down the street, you would see the same tree and the same building over and over. While watching one particular episode of the show, I noticed that Fat Albert walked past the bank. Then a few seconds later, he walked past the bank again. Maybe I had seen too many episodes of *Starsky and Hutch*, but after he past the same bank three times, I realized what was going down. "He's casing the joint. Albert's gonna rob the bank!"

And what was the fascination with black people and trash on television in the 1970s? *Sanford and Son*. Another show with a garbage/junk background.

"Ted. I have this idea for a sitcom starring Redd Foxx. He and his son are junk dealers in Watts. And they get into all kinds of hilarious situations. Maybe there's a neighbor that . . ."

"Stop right there Bill. You've got niggers and trash. What more do you need? That's comedy gold."

I think there was actually a show called *Niggers and Trash* on CBS for a half a season or so in 1978. If I'm not mistaken, it came on right after *The Bob Newhart Show*.

Then there was Oscar the Grouch. He lived in a trash can. Was he black too? No, anyone who ever watched *Sesame Street* knows that Oscar is green. So we know he's not black. And we know he isn't Hispanic because there would have been more than one grouch in that trash can. I can just hear The Count now. "One, two, three, four . . . four Puerto Rican grouches in the trash can. Ah, ha ha haaa!" Relax Puerto Rican readers. Don't we let it slide when you use nigger every now and then? Let's just call it even.

Every now and then I perform a little ritual to rid myself of all the racist and exploitative images that I've seen on television during my lifetime. I'll watch the mini-series *Roots* in reverse.

That way, it has a happy ending. "Yeah! They made it back home!"

At this point, you're probably thinking, "But Nick. There's an entire network dedicated to black programming." Right. How could I forget Black Entertainment Television? Black Entertainment Television bills itself as being a network that is by and for black people. Cool, so what do we get to see? Hard-hitting journalism with stories pertinent to my people? Nope. Quality original programming that doesn't perpetuate the same old Hollywood stereotypes? Nope. How about shows highlighting the more intriguing stories of black culture and history? Nope.

We get to see music videos that feature extreme close-ups of women with ridiculously large backsides. We get to see infomercials. Lots and lots of infomercials. (Did you know that there was a product to de-shell a hard-boiled egg?) We get to see episodes of "classic" black sitcoms. But not the great ones like *The Cosby Show* or *Julia*. We get to see *227* and *Moesha*. We get minstrel show-level stand-up comedy. We get knock-offs of shows like MTV's *Cribs* and *Total Request Live*, without MTV's production skill or budget. In short we get second rate television. And this comes from someone who understands television, OK?

I grew up watching television. Many of my earliest memories involve television. I mean how many people can say that they remember not going with their mother to her weekly bowling league night so that you could stay home and watch the series premiere of *The Incredible Hulk* with their father?

I've spent almost my entire professional career working in different genres and aspects of television. BET is just plain bad. Just look at the production values for example. I remember watching a talk show on BET and thinking "Is someone standing in front of the camera? Why is there a shadow directly on the talent?" Videos are routinely interrupted by commercials. The graphics look like they were produced on an old Commodore 64 computer. The show *Rap City: The Basement* looks like it was actually shot in someone's basement. And not in some hip, *Eight Is Enough* TV basement. It looks like the basement of someone in your family. I think the old stairmaster and tricycle are visible on screen.

The only reason that people don't really talk about the production values of BET is because their programming is so frighteningly bad, that you don't even notice anything else. I don't have any problem with the network featuring music prominently on their schedule. The network began as an entirely music endeavor. Music is an enormous part of black culture. But they have the entire breadth of black music to draw from, and they ignore most of it. Only passing attention is paid to jazz, blues and gospel, but for the most part they focus on hip-hop and modern R&B. And not even the good stuff. They endlessly promote the DMXs and R. Kellys of the music world while better, more positive artists get little or no airplay.

Instead of producing a music video designed to showcase new talent or highlight the work of underappreciated music legends, they created the show *BET Late Night* which features only the raunchiest of the raunchy videos. How's that for serving the black community? You want to see big asses? We got a whole show full of asses just for you.

They get a talented, progressive brother like Tavis Smiley who is interested in producing quality television, and they fire him the second they're taken over by Viacom. Old Tavis is the type of Negro that might step out of line. And the boss doesn't like that one bit.

It might seem a bit presumptuous of me to make all of these statements about BET. After spending time as an employee, I can tell you that the entire corporation deserves every negative thing that is ever said about them. They've earned it.

In 2000, a producer that I had worked with closely during my time at *The Roseanne Show*—the doomed talk show, not the classic sitcom—was given the job of producing the revamped version of BET's late night talk show, *BET Live*. She brought me on board, and I worked as a writer's assistant and eventually became a staff writer. We all came in with the intentions of doing a classy, top-notch talk show. What we got was a lesson in how BET operates.

Most networks try to produce shows that will grab the attention of the major cultural and media centers of the country. Cities like New York, Los Angeles, Chicago, Washington, D.C., and Atlanta. Not BET. Their focus is on placating "the box." The box is the rectangular area that encompasses the entire Deep South. That's their target demographic. I'm sorry if this sounds like I'm practicing geographic prejudice, but when has the Deep South ever been the barometer of cultural signifi-cance? I should know. I was born and raised there. You might ask how I got this little nugget of information. The entire writing staff got this directly from a BET executive.

During one of the staff meetings, someone complained that our bits were too like Jay Leno or David Letterman. We were so shocked that it was actually funny to us, and I'm pretty sure our head writer even laughed out loud. Silly us. Trying to do the things that have been staples of the talk show format for gener-ations. The hardest that I ever made our head writer laugh was when we were having a discussion about the quality of the network. He remarked that they had no desire to improve their programming because they were already getting their target demographic. I told him that they should change their slogan to, "BET. These niggers are watching anyway."

It would almost be easier to rip the network if they were just incompetent. But that's not enough for BET. They're incompetent *and* cheap. Bad combination. I could tell you stories of wardrobe people having to use their own credit cards to buy clothes for talent because BET's credit wasn't accepted at major department stores. I could tell you stories about a lighting director who threatened to have his crew take down all the lights— essentially halting production—if he wasn't paid immediately. Because of that, our line producer was forced to ask the people in an upper level staff meeting, with a straight face, if he could borrow thirty thousand dollars. I could tell you stories of waiting around late on payday because our paychecks just hadn't shown up yet. I could tell you stories of being discouraged from writing jokes about the president for fear of upsetting the Democratic Party. The first page of the textbook in Talk Show 101 is *Chapter 1: Make Fun of the President.* As if the DNC watches BET anyway. But I won't tell you any of those stories because that would be overkill. But, I will tell you one story that most accurately depicts their preposterously parsimonious ways. They stiffed their host on his paycheck.

First, a little background information. If you've ever been a little short when it came time to pay the bills, you've probably tried this trick. You have a telephone bill due, but not enough money in the bank to cover it. So, to buy some time, you write out a check for the amount, but you don't sign the check. No personal check is valid without a signature, so the telephone company is forced to send you another invoice, effectively giving you an extra week to pay the bill. Now, back to our story. As most talk show hosts do, John Salley spent a fair amount of time hanging out in the writers' room. The relaxed, laid-back nature of the people in the room combined with the fact that we weren't bashful about showing our overall distaste for the network led to a tremendous amount of candor in our conversations. John Salley told us the following story.

For tax purposes, Salley's paycheck was to be made out to his corporation and not to him personally. After his initial few paychecks, he believed that the problem had been solved. Then, several weeks into production, it happened again. When his agent called him to explain that they had made the check out to him personally again, John had an idea. Instead of returning it to BET, he had his agent go ahead and deposit the check. There were insufficient funds in BET's account to cover the amount of his paycheck. Sound familiar?

My frustration with BET as a network is compounded by the success of Telemundo and Univision. Catering to the Latin population, these networks boast a roster of original shows that span all genres. Their programming consists of original comedies and dramas, including their immensely popular soap operas known as telenovelas. They also have variety shows, talk shows, and original sports programming. They also manage to have an incredibly beautiful woman on the screen at all times. Even during their news programs. Flipping through the channels you might stop and think, "Why is Ms. Puerto Rico interviewing Colin Powell?" She's not. Their anchorwomen are just that hot. Aye fucking caramba. Every straight man that I know has watched thirty minutes of programming in a foreign language just because there were really pretty women on screen. I don't know what happened on *Six Feet Under* last week, but I can give you the extended weather forecast for Guadalajara.

This may be straying just a bit off topic, but I cannot, in good conscience, talk so extensively about television without mentioning one of the most overlooked issues of the entire 1980s. I call it the Conrad Bain effect. The television show *Diff'rent Strokes* serves as the perfect example of two important Hollywood phenomena. The first being the use of cute kids to attract viewers. The second being the cautionary tale of young actors getting too much too soon. The entire success of the show was based upon the freakishly adorable Gary Coleman. Coleman was born with a congenital kidney disease that caused his incredibly shortened stature. Instead of being a setback, his affliction helped to launch his career. Coleman was three and a half feet of concentrated cuteness. He exhibited a precociousness that Hollywood hadn't seen since Shirley Temple, and he didn't even have to tap dance to entertain. Gary Coleman was so popular that America demanded a second tiny, adorable, diseased black boy on television. *Webster* star Emmanuel Lewis was even shorter and his cheeks more pinchable than Gary. Gary Coleman was so popular that America tolerated him even after he entered into the unfortunate less-adorable years that so many child actors face. (Let's be honest. For a while there, *The Cosby Show*'s Keshia Knight Pulliam was just plain scary looking.) The *E! True Hollywood Story* on *Diff'rent Strokes* revealed the fact that at one point in the show's run Coleman was undergoing dialysis treatment multiple times a week. He was a ten-year-old kid carrying a hit sitcom on his back, all while he was seriously ill. Remember that shit the next time you want to use Gary as the punch line to a joke or you call in sick to work.

But the most talked about aspect of *Diff'rent Strokes* is, of course, the downfall of all three of the show's young stars. Coleman was forced to sue his parents over misappropriation of his $3.8 million trust fund. Despite this, he declared bankruptcy in 1999. In 2000, he was charged with assault and ordered to pay bus driver Tracy Fields $1,665 for her hospital bills that resulted from a fight. Fields had asked Coleman for an autograph while he was shopping for a bulletproof vest. Yes. I said bulletproof vest. Fuck 50 Cent. Li'l GC was way ahead of his time. The video of Coleman explaining that he felt "threatened by her insistence" and saw no other recourse other than to jump up and punch her in the head is funnier than all of the best episodes of *Diff'rent Strokes* combined.

Gary's television brother Todd Bridges turned it up a notch with his post-series troubles. After three auto-related incidents—threatening to blow up a detailer, reckless driving, and not paying a $500 repair bill—Bridges graduated to the big leagues when he was arrested on suspicion of shooting and stabbing alleged drug dealer Kenneth Clay in a Los Angeles crack house. Apparently, after Bridges confessed that he couldn't pay for his drugs, Clay inquired as to what he was talking about "Willis." Bridges snapped. Thanks to his defense attorney, Johnnie Cochran—talk about foreshadowing—Bridges was acquitted of assault with a deadly weapon. After his acquittal, Bridges was promptly accused of . . . stabbing his roommate. The rest of his bio is standard Hollywood fare. He developed a coke habit, got busted for gun possession, found God, got clean, and made a semi-comeback.

The saddest story stemming from the show is the tale of Dana Plato. Plato was fired from *Diff'rent Strokes* after she became pregnant. As her career slumped, she resorted to appearing in soft-core pornography and developed drug and alcohol problems. She was arrested in 1991 for robbing a video store in Las Vegas, but was placed on probation. The following year, she was arrested again, this time for forging a prescription for Valium. In 1999, she died of an overdose from the painkiller Loritab and the muscle relaxant Valium. Her death was ruled a suicide.

Now ask yourself one question. What did these three people have in common? That's right. Conrad Bain. I find it curious that when people speak of all three of these fallen child stars, a myriad of other influences is listed as a potential cause for their plight. Drugs, showbiz excess, sexual abuse, greedy parents, yet no one seems willing to point the finger at the obvious choice. I've got my eye on you Conrad.

Chapter 13

An Open Letter to
Mel Gibson*

Tuesday, August 24, 2004

Mr. Mel Gibson
c/o Alan Nierob
Rogers & Cowan Ltd Advertising
(310) 201-8800
1888 Century Park East
5th Floor
Los Angeles, CA 90067

Dear Mr. Gibson,

Now that the uproar over your very successful movie, The Passion of the Christ, *has passed, I thought it would be a good time to point out a glaring oversight in the accuracy of the film.*

You have been quoted as saying that you simply wanted to tell the story as it's told in The Bible. *You said that the gospel is the complete script, and that's what you filmed. Well, if you've read the script then of course you realize that you cast the wrong actor to play Jesus Christ. I'm sure you're aware that*

*Actual letter mailed to Mel Gibson.

The Bible *tells us that Jesus "had hair like lambs wool and feet the color of brass as if they've been burned in a furnace." Now I'm not a biblical scholar, but I can tell a dark skinned man with a Jew-fro when I see it. Obviously, Jim Caviezel does not fit that description. Since you are a true Christian who is dedicated to giving people the word of* The Bible *in its purest form, I'm sure you will realize your mistake and take all the necessary steps to rectify your error. I look forward to the release of the special edition DVD with a re-cast lead playing the role of Jesus. Perhaps a well-tanned Gabe Kaplan or Jeff Goldblum?*

P.S.
The Road Warrior *was awesome.*

Yours in Christ,

Nick Adams

Chapter 14

Top 5 Movie Deaths by Black Actors

One of the biggest clichés surrounding race in Hollywood is that the black guy in the movie always dies first. It was never completely accurate. In horror movies, for example, the correct order is slut, asshole guy, *then* black guy. In recent years, this observation has become less relevant. (Spend a few months in a tiny editing room watching Keanu Reeves and Laurence Fishburne on screen at the same time. I dare you to kill off Morpheus in the first act.) Slowly, but surely the old adage seems to be going the way of the dinosaur. So, I thought it would be fitting to celebrate the five most glorious screen deaths by black actors. Warning; if you haven't seen these movies, you may want to skip this section since there are major spoilers. Also, you might want to climb out of that cinematic hole you've been living in and take your ass to Blockbuster or get a Netflix account.

#5 Jim Brown

The Dirty Dozen

First things first. Best dick flick ever. Period. (Dick flick is the male counterpart to chick flick. When you're sick of reading that term in *Entertainment Weekly*, remember to blame me for making it up. Or at least being the first one to claim it.) Every man should be forced to see this movie before they're allowed to go through puberty. You wanna ejaculate? Fine. Watch this movie first. Then we'll talk about letting you become a man. *The Dirty Dozen* was released way before my time, but I'm sure that I had the same reaction as black moviegoers did when the movie came out back in 1967.

"He's gonna make it. He's gonna make it. Aw shit. He didn't make it."

We all hated to see him get it at the end of the movie. But if he had to go out, at least he went out like a hero. The image of Jim Brown sprinting across the screen, dodging enemy fire, is one of the most breathtaking scenes in the history of American cinema. It's right up there with that slow motion shot of Phoebe Cates coming out of the pool in *Fast Times at Ridgemont High*.

The second best thing about the movie is the one man creep-fest put on by Donald Sutherland. So *that's* where Keifer got it from.

#4 Samuel L. Jackson

Deep Blue Sea

The only remotely interesting scene in an otherwise forget-table film. Not even the always entertaining Michael Rapaport could save this movie. Not even a scantily clad Saffron Burrows could save this movie. Not even the impeccable acting skill of Stellan Skarsgård—*Dancer in the Dark, Good Will Hunting, Ronin, Amistad, Insomnia, The Hunt for Red October*—could save this movie. You know there is something fundamentally wrong with a movie that kills off Samuel L. Jackson's character but lets LL Cool J's character live to the end. Still, I recommend that you watch it up until the one-hour-and-nine-second mark so you can see Samuel L. go out in a blaze of gory. No, not glory. Gory.

If you haven't seen the movie—lucky you—it's about genetically engineered smart sharks. (I know, I know. It even sounds horrible. I think these are the same guys behind *Cocktail*.) After the shark's initial attacks, the characters gather together to regroup. They're all totally freaked out and Sam is attempting to rally the troops using his best Jules Winfield voice. Stay calm and we'll all get out of here alive, blah blah blah. As he's delivering his speech he's standing dangerously close to the water's edge. I remember thinking, "Get away from the water, Sam." Sure enough, one of the super sharks leaps out of the water onto the platform and drags Sam, kicking and screaming, into the ocean. It's not believable. The CGI is pretty bad. And it's fucking awesome. It's one of those holy shit movie moments where you find yourself yelling at the screen. (Remember the first time you saw *The Karate Kid*? "He's doing the crane thing!" It's like that.) The only way it could have been cooler is if the shark had recited a Bible verse before he ate him.

#3 The Black Guy

Saving Private Ryan

Oops. There weren't any black people in *Saving Private Ryan*. Despite the fact that they were still being treated like second class citizens at home, over 400,000 black soldiers served in World War II. Thanks for ignoring us, Steve.

#2 Charles S. Dutton

Alien³

Another highlight in a lowlight of a movie. The only thing that prevents *Alien³* from receiving more scorn is *Alien: Resurrection*. (Seriously, Winona Ryder? Worst casting ever.) In the third installment of the *Alien* series, Ridley awakens on a prison colony with two of the creatures. One roaming loose and the other growing inside her. In an effort to trap the full-grown alien, Charles S. Dutton's character must hold the creature off while Ripley climbs up and pours a few thousand gallons of molten lead onto the beast. Clichéd? Yes. Predictable? Yes. But Dutton makes it work. Taunting the Alien into the trap, Dutton screams, "Fuck you. Come on. Is that all you got? Is that as hard as you can bite, motherfucker!" He's still spitting like a cornered alley cat as he engages the deadliest creature in the known universe in hand-to-hand combat that he knows will lead to certain death. Maybe it's the knowledge that Dutton served seven years in prison for stabbing a man in a street fight that made me think he at least stood a fighting chance.

#1 The 54th Regiment of Massachusetts Voluntary Infantry

Glory

Around Oscar time, you always hear terms like "triumph of the human spirit" and "heart wrenching" being thrown around. *Glory* is the kind of movie for which terms like that should be reserved. The movie is full of captivating scenes. (Denzel being whipped for going AWOL should also be required viewing for every adult male.) Technically, the scene that I'm referring to isn't a death scene. It's a night before death scene. Basically, Matthew Broderick's character has volunteered himself and his group of former slaves to lead an assault on Ft. Wagner. The climactic sequence is magnificent, but ultimately futile. Most of the regiment died in the battle, including all of the movie's main characters. Ft. Wagner was never captured. But the singing and praying that takes place among the soldiers the night before the battle always brings me to the verge of tears. In a movie about men fighting for their very freedom, it can all be summed up with Denzel Washington's character saying, "Ain't much a matter what happens tomorrow. We men ain't we?" Too bad America didn't agree.

Chapter 15

Not Necessarily
the News

As I mentioned before, I got my start in television working as a Desk Assistant at NBC News in Washington, D.C. I was excited about starting in the real world and was generally unfazed by what was quite an intimidating job. You started working at the assignment desk, manning about eight phone lines and three fax machines. All of which were working nonstop from the early morning until after the nightly broadcast aired. Once you gained experience, they would assign you to work other tasks around the bureau. After a few months, I had amassed some D.A. seniority, and spent less time on the desk. From time to time, I would join in on one of the favorite newsroom practices. Standing around the television and discussing whatever was going on in the world. I have a distinct memory of walking into the newsroom and seeing that now-familiar headshot of a beaming, blond JonBenet Ramsey. Without thinking, I said out loud to no one in particular, "Why is it news that this little white girl is dead?" I was greeted with silence which I read as disinterest. I kept on walking and left the newsroom. Years later, I ask the question again. Why was it national news when JonBenet Ramsey was killed? Everyday, all across the country, little brown babies, and yellow babies, and red babies and black babies get abducted or murdered and not one of them has become a major national story. I'm afraid that if a little Filipino girl had fallen down the well instead of baby Jessica, she'd still be down there.

Let's start with JonBenet. First of all, it did not fit the criteria of being national news. News is generally defined as something that is interesting and relevant to the reader or viewer. Obviously, the death of a child in Boulder, Colorado, isn't really relevant to most people in the country. It's horrible, but it's not affecting their lives. So, maybe every editor and news director in the free world thought that there was something more interesting with this murder than all the other children who were killed that same week or month. There was. Those damn headshots. You remember them. She was posed just so, like some sort of hyper-sexualized, modern-day Shirly Temple. America was transfixed. White people were captivated by this ultra-WASPY über-baby and horrified by what her parents had done to her. (Here's a hint parents. Your six-year-old daughter should never look like a whore.)

Were it not for those pictures, the story wouldn't have made a blip on the radar screen of the twenty-four-hour news channels. If you take away the sensational angle of the story—which is what journalists are supposed to do, right?—you're left with a pretty run-of-the-mill homicide. Little girl found murdered in the basement. Parents suspected. Nothing ever proved. That story is no more newsworthy than a story about a little black girl who gets killed by a stray bullet in the Southeast section of D.C. It's no more newsworthy than a story about a little Hispanic girl who gets hit by a drunk driver as she's jumping rope on the sidewalk in Long Beach. How many important stories do you think never saw the light of day because we were getting the latest JonBenet update? Thousands. Given all the things that the networks don't tell us about politics, world affairs, the environment, the business world and health care . . . I'd say that is a very conservative estimate. Wouldn't it be more important to tell people about how big corporations are benefiting from the IMF and the World Bank's privatization of the natural resources of South American countries? If you live in Peru, you wake up one morning and can't afford clean drinking water. Or, how about you do a news story on the news itself? In his book, *Crimes Against Nature*, Robert F. Kennedy Jr. writes, "The FCC rule that forbids ownership of more than one TV station in any market has been broken in 43 cities surveyed by the Center for Public Integrity." In Wilmington, North Carolina, one media company basically controls the three news stations. Those are two important, interesting stories that don't see the light of day because CNN has a thing for really young blondes.

My favorite tidbit from the entire JonBenet story involves her creepy parents. I remember watching a news report that mentioned that, so far, the parents had declined to talk to the police. Declined? How did they ever even have a choice? I wonder if a black couple's daughter had been found murdered in their basement, if they would have been given the option of whether or not they wanted to speak to the police. And wouldn't any parents in their right minds be more than willing to sit down with the police and answer any questions they might have with the hopes that it would bring their daughter's killer to justice? Very shady. As for the police in Boulder, it doesn't say very much for their crime-solving skills. This case was the only murder in their city for the entire year. It was also one of the highest profile murder cases in decades. It remains unsolved. If the cops couldn't crack this one, the residents of Boulder can pretty much forget about ever seeing their various stolen wallets, bicycles, and cars again. Just so we're clear, I'm not making light of her murder. It was a horrible crime. I'm just trying to understand the mind-set of a country that grieves more for children of one color than it does for those of another.

To me, the news story that most easily encapsulates America's feeling toward black youths would be the way the school shootings were handled. In the late 1990s there was a succession of highly publicized school shootings. Shootings in West Paducah, Kentucky, and Jonesboro, Arizona, both received massive amounts of coverage but it was the Columbine High School shooting in Littleton, Colorado, that really sent the press, and subsequently the nation, into a panic. All of a sudden, white suburban parents were worried about their children's safety every time they went to school. Although statistics showed that violent crimes among teenagers were steadily declining, the safety of America's children became everyone's focus. I don't want to sound jealous or anything, but black kids have been shooting each other for years and nobody gave a damn. You could get all the Crips and all the Bloods in the entire city of Los Angeles and wage a huge battle in the parking lot of Channel 4 News. The local anchors would walk through the parking lot stepping over fresh bodies only to sit down at the news desk, look at the camera and say, "Today's top story: Sean Connery has hip replacement surgery. News 4's Ted Chen is live at Cedars Sinai Hospital."

Oh sure, there was that brief period of time in the early 1990s after John Singleton's *Boyz n the Hood* came to multiplexes all over the country and people were suddenly concerned with the lives of black youths in the inner city. During that time, the outrage wasn't over why these kids were so alienated that they felt the need to join a gang for a feeling of protection and sense of family. It wasn't about understanding the culture that could make a young black male think that violence and crime were the only ways that he could achieve some level of success. It wasn't about wondering how these young, civilian men could get their hands on automatic pistols and assault weapons. More than anything else, it was about putting niggers in jail. Period. They didn't want to understand why people were gang-banging and selling crack cocaine. They just wanted to lock them up for it. And lock them up they did. White people went into overdrive and began drafting and implementing three-strikes laws, upping mandatory sentencing, increasing police budgets so they could buy assault vehicles and automatic rifles. OK. Fine. You want to be conservative when it comes to crime—even among those under eighteen—I can understand that. What I don't understand is why that same feeling doesn't apply to white kids who commit the same violent crime. When some middle-class white kid decides to take a gun to school and kill as many of his classmates as possible, everyone suddenly becomes a bleeding-heart liberal. Why did these kids do this? We need to understand the mind-set of these troubled youths. What's causing our kids to have this disconnect with reality? Is it the violent video games? Is it action movies like *The Matrix?* We need to have tougher gun control in this country. Is it even safe to send my child to school?

Let's indulge this thinking for a minute. Why did these troubled youths suddenly snap? What horrible things were occurring in the lives of Columbine High School students Eric Harris and Dylan Klebold? The only thing that might suggest something out of the ordinary is that Harris had been rejected by the Marines because he was taking the antidepressant Luvox. As far as I can tell, they were pretty normal kids with a mother and father present in both households. There is no evidence of abuse at home. Combined, they were involved in the Boy Scouts, Little League, and their school's news network. It doesn't seem that they were that ostracized from their classmates since both sets of parents say that their sons had active social lives. They played video games, went bowling, and were involved in fantasy football leagues. Even though the two wrote about not fitting in and not being accepted, most of the people that they plotted against— jocks, girls who had rejected them—were unaware that they had ever done anything to offend either of the two. Basically, these two were just really big nerds.

If what I'm about to say offends anyone, I apologize in advance. Fuck those two. Yes, you read correctly. Fuck them. I have absolutely zero sympathy for those two. Eric Harris and Dylan Klebold were children of privilege. The median household income for Littleton is $50,000. The Littleton school system has a graduation rate of 96%. If you can't handle the pressures of a suburban, middle-class high school, then you're probably better off locked up in a cell somewhere anyway. So you're a nerd? Big deal. Just hang out with the other nerds. Find the least unattractive nerd girl and take her to the prom. It's just high school. These kids had to realize that this wasn't the end-all and be-all of their lives, right? Hell, Klebold had already been accepted into the University of Arizona. In fact, the family had driven to Arizona only a month before the shootings to pick out his dorm room. (Perhaps, the thought of spending August in Tucson was too much for him to take? After all, I can speak from experience having served two years there while my wife was in graduate school. One hundred fourteen degrees is hot enough to make anyone snap.) I'm sure he could have sucked it up for a few more months. When you get to college, they don't call you a nerd anymore. They call you the band. But at least you get to hang out with other band members and get drunk before the football games. And once you've graduated from college and moved on to the workforce, they have another name for the people who were nerds in high school. Boss. Have you seen Bill Gates? One look at that guy and you just know he got more than his fair share of wedgies as a schoolboy.

Compare their "struggles" to those of some less fortunate youngsters in the country. If there's a black kid whose father is out of the picture and his mom is working two jobs and barely making ends meet, what do you expect him to say when his old friend asks him if wants to make some quick cash by robbing a liquor store? If there's a Mexican kid watching his parents break their backs doing domestic work and day labor, what is he going to say when someone asks if he'll drive a few kilos of marijuana and cocaine across the border in a pickup truck? The same people who cried crocodile tears over the dead bodies at Columbine turn a blind eye to these stories, and to the social problems that cause them, every single day. The message that is being sent here is loud and clear. Our children are more important than yours.

But this isn't new. White people have a long history of ignoring an issue until it smacks them right in the face. Rap music had violent lyrics for years, but it wasn't until white children started listening to the music that anyone gave a damn about the messages that were contained in the songs. Voilà! Explicit lyrics stickers on albums. God forbid that Karenna Gore could listen to a little Ice-T without Tipper getting her panties all in a bunch. Nobody cared about the drug problem when heroin was destroying the black community in the 1960s and '70s. And they ignored the crack epidemic in the 1980s until it crossed to their side of the tracks. Voilà! Just say no. (Seriously. Is that the best they could do?) We did the same thing with violence among our youth. In America, a problem isn't a problem until it's a problem to white people. *Then* it's a problem.

Chapter 16

Black and White. Not Read All Over

The same separate-but-equal policy that applies in Hollywood is also what keeps classic black literature marginalized. Let's say you go into Borders or Barnes and Noble and you're looking for Zora Neale Hurston's *Their Eyes Were Watching God*, or James Baldwin's *The Fire Next Time*. It seems like the obvious thing to do would be to go into the fiction department and search for the author's last name, right? Wrong. I guess those two giants of American literature aren't important enough to share the same shelves as Ernest Hemingway and Saul Bellow. They have to be relegated to the book ghetto. Tucked away in a tiny corner of the store right next to the Gay & Lesbian fiction section. (It's a similar setup in most cities. There's the good neighborhood. Waspy. Kind of sterile. Head east and you get to the neighborhood where all the gay people live. A little less homogenous, but still nice. And much hipper. Cool. Keep going east and you get to the black neighborhood. White people don't want to be in that neighborhood unless they're eating soul food or buying weed. I don't even buy my weed in the black neighborhoods. I get my weed

139

from a fifty-year-old white guy with a ponytail who lives in the valley.)

I'm sure the public relations departments of the big book sellers would tell you that this is to make it easier to find the black authors. Bullshit. What's easier than just listing them alphabetically under the author's last name? That would be less work for the store and less work for the customer. Putting them in a separate section also makes them less likely to be read. The black person who's going into Brentano's to rediscover Richard Wright is going to find *Native Son* no matter what. But what about the white reader who decides to search the shelves for an old classic that they have never gotten around to reading? That person will probably just go to the fiction section and begin browsing until they find something that tickles their fancy. By doing this, they might just happen upon *The Great Gatsby* or *Look Homeward, Angel*, but unless they venture over to the south side of the store, they probably won't ever think to read *The Invisible Man*. Hell, if Oprah Winfrey hadn't made *The Bluest Eye* a selection for her book club, most of white America would still think that Toni Morrison was a character on *General Hospital*. Since you are already reading my book, perhaps you will go a step further and do me a favor. Go back to the store where you bought this book, grab all the copies from the shelf, and put them up front and center next to the new John Grisham book. (Let me guess. It's about a lawyer, right?) While you're at it, buy five more copies of the book.

At least a small percentage of white folks will know something about writers of color. Either by taking an African-American literature class in college or just having a high school teacher or university professor progressive enough to include books by black writers in their curriculum. There are also the

Beckys and Megans of the world who are going out with a black guy and want to understand his struggle. (Becky. Megan. Do yourself, and him, a favor. Don't read *Invisible Man*. You will get a headache. Your man will just get annoyed. "Being invisible would be so awesome. Like, I could totally go into Erin's room and see if she's been talking about me behind my back. And if she was, I would like just push her down. Just totally push her and run out of the room. Awesome.")

Even if these books are considered classics of black fiction, at least they are considered classics and there are some people who will always treat them as such. What about the current crop of black fiction writers? I'm not talking about those people writing in this bullshit genre of pseudo-black fiction. That stuff turns my stomach. You know the books I'm talking about. They are written by authors who use all three of their names because they think that makes them sound literary. They have horrible, glossy, illustrated covers of muscular black men embracing curvaceous black women. They have titles like *Sister Girl's Blues* or *Soul Man*. The protagonists of these novels—if they can even be called novels—are usually executives at record labels or editors at cheesy hip-hop or R&B magazines and live lifestyles of lavish music video excess. Whereas serious novels contain themes like alienation, redemption, or coming to terms with one's past, these books are content to tackle the issue of how LaVonda can get her baby's daddy to do the right thing. No, my concern isn't for these books. They're going to have a shot because they're prominently displayed front and center in your local bookstore. These authors will be fine because the book-reading public has shown an amazing ability to choose work that caters to the lowest common denominator. They'll purchase and read these horrible, horrible books even though they would probably get more

Nick Adams

intellectual stimulation if they just tore the pages up, sprinkled them with feta cheese, doused them in a light vinaigrette, and ate them.

I'm concerned with people like Percival Everett, ZZ Packer, and Jamaica Kincaid. These and other black authors who are actually attempting to write books of substance are being largely overlooked by the book-buying public because they don't fit into the nice little niche that the mega chains would like them to. I don't think it's a coincidence that Zadie Smith just happens to be British and has striking good looks. If she was just a sister from Atlanta who wrote a thoughtful, hilarious book that was, in part, a sweeping indictment of Anglo-Saxon imperialism, I doubt that she would have received the universal praise that she did for *White Teeth*. I sent my sister, who can be a voracious reader, a copy of Stephen L. Carter's *The Emperor of Ocean Park* and she reported back that she didn't like it because the author was "too pleased with himself." Well, the guy is a Stanford- and Yale-educated law professor who clerked for Thurgood Marshall and wrote an amazing debut novel that was adored by almost every major book critic. Shouldn't he feel just a little pleased with himself? As I write this, I'm not even finished with my semi-intellectual indictment of race relations and pop culture in America and I'm already quite pleased with myself.

For some reason, black authors aren't rewarded for intellectualism in the same way that white authors are. (But then again, you could substitute the word "people" for the word "authors" in that last sentence couldn't you?) And black readers haven't yet realized that you should expect a little bit of pretension from their literature. Writing itself is pretentious. Think about the arrogance required for someone to think, "I am going to take all of these clever stories and ideas that I have in my head and put

142

them all on paper. People will spend their hard-earned money to read my brilliant ideas." What an arrogant bastard! And I proudly count myself among that number. That's what being creative is about. That's the inherent risk and reward of taking this path. Every singer, writer, actor, comedian, poet, or artist of any real integrity goes to bed every night thinking that they have something special and unique to give to the world. When times get really tough and you start to wish that you had taken the more secure route, that belief is the only thing that you have to cling to. That belief breeds more work, which breeds a better artist, which breeds more pretension. Oddly enough, that sort of earned arrogance is understood and appreciated within some forms of media or art, but not others. We understand the cocky athlete. We understand the macho rap or R&B star. We don't understand the overly multisyllabic, slightly eccentric novelist. As a result, we don't really understand their writing. So, we don't read their books. We've successfully dumbed down literature like we've dumbed down every other aspect of our country. That's why so many people identified with George W. Bush. He's functionally illiterate just like the rest of the country.

Imagine you're a novelist and you happen to be black. You've written for your entire life. You went to an excellent university and a top-notch graduate school to get your Masters of Fine Arts in creative writing. After banging out a collection of short stories and a first novel, you publish a sophomore effort that is everything you dreamed your writing could be. It dealt with issues of race, but wasn't necessarily about race. It was no more about race than *Animal Farm* was about livestock. You refuse to compromise or condescend to your reader. Nothing is dumbed down. Maybe it's even downright difficult to read at times. You think it could be the great American novel. And the

critics agree with you. You stride into a bookstore one day, looking forward to that thrill of seeing your book on the shelves.
And as many serious white novelists enjoy the thrill of being
front-and-center in the displays, or in the fiction section alphabetically, you are forced to hunt for the lone African-American
fiction section which is tucked away in a corner. What a knee to
the groin that must be. That's how the book industry rewards
black writers who have the gall to attempt to write something
worth remembering. Something too smart and too complex to
be put into a nice neat little category. It sounds like a little thing,
but that's how racism—yes, it is racism, white reader—operates
these days. See, this isn't some grand plan by the bookstores to
keep the black man down. It's just that this is still the way that
white Americans see people of color. One-dimensional, disposable, cardboard cutouts. Place "ex-con turned do-gooder" here.
Place "sassy secretary" here. Easy, right. Yeah, except then you
run into an honest-to-goodness, real-live black person. And we
don't work that way. You have to interact with us like the falli-
ble, flesh-and-blood, unpredictable human beings that we are.

PART IV

Politics and
Society

Chapter 17

Who Wants to Get Shot?

Whenever someone bemoans the state of black America, someone else points out that the problem is the lack of leadership. My standard response is that given the track record for most black leaders of note, why would anyone be actively seeking that position? How far into the interview do you get before they bring that up?

"Are you a captivating public speaker?"

"Yes."

"Do you look good in a suit?"

"Oh, yes."

"Umm. How do you feel about getting shot in the head?"

"Well, I'd prefer not to if that's OK. I'd be willing to relocate, and I'm flexible on salary, but I'd really rather not get shot in the head."

"Well, we might be able to make an exception just this once. Let me talk to my partners and get back to you on that."

Historically, whenever a black man seemed close to achieving any significant social, political change—either by opposing the system, or changing it from within—he met with an untimely end. The government is really smart about it too. They don't just kill our leaders the second they start getting recognition. That would be too obvious. They wait until just the right time to pull the trigger. If you know your history, you know that Dr. Martin Luther King Jr. had already made a lot of noise in this country by the time 1968 rolled around. Behind him was the bus boycott in Montgomery, Alabama, the freedom rides, and the march on Washington, D.C. During all that time, the powers that be were content with amassing a phone book size file on Dr. King. But as soon as he started focusing his attention on not just race, but nationwide poverty regardless of skin color, alarm bells went off and James Earl Ray went to the bushes.

In what is probably the irony of all ironies, one of the more respected black political figures in the country right now is Al Sharpton. Somehow, when America wasn't looking, Al was able to transform his image from articulate, shady rabble-rouser to articulate, respectable, would-be politician. During the 2004 Democratic debates, he consistently presented the most cogent reasoning, was by far the most compelling speaker, and was incredibly likeable. So what's the problem with Al? It's really hard to have your main spokesperson be someone who's not going to sugarcoat the problem or play nice at all. I never thought I would find myself saying this, but he's *too* black. Al is just extra black all day long. It must be incredibly exhausting to be friends with him. Can you imagine taking the day off and going to the ball park with Al Sharpton?

"Why does Mariano Rivera have to come out of the bullpen? All the white boys get to be starters."

"Al, relax. He's a relief pitcher. That's just the way it is."

"And why is that, brother? Because the white man says that's the way it is. Big Boss Steinbrenner has decreed that it be so, and we should just sit here and take it? Massa say I can't pitch 'til the eighth inning."

He can't be *that* black all day every day can he? That would be so exhausting to be around. I bet that it's just an act. I'll bet you Al Sharpton has spent at least one Saturday curled up on the couch drinking chamomile tea and watching a *Felicity* marathon.

White people are just never going to follow Al Sharpton. Not gonna happen. During the 2004 debates, my best friend— who's a lawyer—told me about a conversation that he kept having with white people.

White person: "Boy that Al Sharpton is sure something. He's the only reason why I watch the debates."

My friend: "So, are you gonna vote for him?"

White person: "Well . . . umm . . . I umm . . . Dick Gephardt . . ."

Al Sharpton was the only remotely interesting thing about each and every Democratic debate and he still had to drop out. Check that. There were a few other entertaining things about the debates, such as: What the hell was Carol Moseley-Braun doing? Seriously Ms. Carol . . . black woman? We have a long way to go before we nominate a black woman for any position that has the words "president" and "United States" in the title. Carol Moseley-Braun would probably have a hard time defeating Robert E. Whitley if she decided to run for president of the United States Tour Operators Association. When it comes to being the president of the whole country, she has to know that she's at least behind "white woman" and "black man" on the minority election list. After all, every person who's ever held the office of President or Vice President has been a white Anglo-

Saxon male. The Democrats nominated a Jew for V.P. in 2000 and the entire Republican Party experienced an incredibly powerful, collective orgasm. My wife and I finally decided that Ms. Moseley-Braun was trying to set herself up for a nice fat cabinet position in case Clark, Dean, or Kerry managed to win. I remember that she took great care not to piss off any of the favorites. "I agree with Governor Dean and by the way, that's a lovely tie you're wearing, Howard."

Dennis Kucinich was good for more than a few laughs. There were just so many reasons why he had no chance in hell. The name. Kucinich? Way too ethnic. And not even specifically ethnic, but nebulously ethnic, which is worse. His name allowed all the bigots in the country to just assume that he belonged to whatever specific group that they held a bias toward, Jews, immigrants, whatever. Kucinich is also a little guy which isn't a good thing for a presidential candidate. James Madison was the shortest president at about 5 feet 4 inches, but there was no CNN in 1809. Madison didn't have to worry about looking like a small child when he stood next to John Jay and Alexander Hamilton. (Side note. The White House Web site actually describes Madison's wife, Dolly, as buxom. Does anyone else find it odd that they would reference her breasts on a government site?

Kucinich does support the decriminalization of marijuana which won him some bonus points in the household of a certain comedian/writer and his wife. That's right. Al and Franni Franken smoke copious amounts of marijuana.

One of the most frustrating things about this never-ending search for a black leader is that there is a man of African descent who holds one of the most respected positions in the world and carries himself like a natural born statesman. Just our luck that he also happens to be from Ghana and not the United States. I am, of course, referring to the Secretary General of the United Nations, Kofi Annan. He is probably the most powerful minority figure in the world, and although he's not actually African-American, I think we should go ahead and claim him. Tiger Woods is more Thai than anything and black folks everywhere bent over backward trying to take credit for his success. Why not bring Kofi into the fold as well? Hell, he even looks the part. Kind of like an older, better-groomed version of Danny Glover. Let's hope that he's not getting too old for this shit. The problem is that most people—black or otherwise—in this country have no idea who Kofi Annan is. If you were to ask three random people who Kofi Annan was, you'd get three totally different answers.

"Kofi Annan? Yeah I know who that guy is. He played power forward for the Pistons. Solid defender. Good rebounder. I think he went to Washington State, right?"

"Do I know Kofi Annan? Shit, man, I got all his albums. The early acoustic stuff. The jazz fusion stuff he was doing before he died. I saw him open up for Hugh Masekela in 1972."

"Kofi Annan's? Oh, that's the little Ethiopian restaurant down on Fairfax. That place is excellent. You know they have live jazz there on Sunday nights, right?"

As much as I respect the organization and the man, I have to admit he has an extremely lame title. Secretary General? First of all, it makes no sense. He's not a secretary and it's not a military position. Plus, making secretary part of the title for what is an extremely important job is kind of disrespectful. It's the ultimate backhanded compliment. It's like when a pimp calls one of his working girls his "#1 'ho."

One of the things that frustrates me about the black people is that we consistently fight the wrong battles. A few years back, the topic of reparations attracted a lot of heat from mainstream media and black intellectuals. I couldn't help but think to myself, "Why the fuck are we even talking about this. This is never going to happen." Seriously, there is absolutely, 100%, no chance whatsoever of black people ever being given reparations for slavery. What makes us think that the government would be willing to pay us back for the worst indignity that we were forced to endure, when they haven't even bothered to apologize or attempted to make amends for the smaller ones? The Tuskegee experiment. Smuggling heroin from Southeast Asia directly into the black community. Disenfranchisement in Florida during the 2000 election. Why not try to cut some checks for those things first? Hell, I'd be happy if someone would just apologize for the TV show *Homeboys in Outer Space*. (And while we're on the subject of white people apologizing, Mickey Rooney still owes one to the entire Asian community. Just rent *Breakfast at Tiffany's* and you'll see what I'm talking about.) White people are *never* going to repay us for slavery. Never. I think my little *Amistad* theory from earlier already proved that they don't like being reminded of slavery. There's no way they're going to give black people money for it.

But back to my point. If black people want to keep making progress in this country, we have to fight the more important battles first. Every year, the NAACP makes a big stink about the lack of minorities on television and in movies. Now, as someone who has worked extensively behind the camera and has on-camera aspirations, I'm concerned about this as well. But with all the other, more pressing issues facing black America, I'm surprised that the NAACP even has time to address this one. When you think about the fact that there are more black men in prison than in college, does it really matter how many black people are on *CSI: Miami*? We're pissed off because they aren't enough black people playing lawyers on television when we should be pissed off because there aren't enough black people going to law school in real life.

White Americans treat all minorities like the boy who cried wolf. If you raise too much of a stink over something that isn't that big of a deal, they'll only ignore you when you try to bring more serious issues to their attention.

I'm making light of this situation, but I really mean what I'm saying. When are black people going to realize what the word "minority" means? Nowhere is the definition more painfully obvious than in Hollywood. I know, because I've seen it. I've been inside the offices of big time Hollywood agencies and inside the offices of broadcast and cable networks. You know what I saw? White people. Lots and lots of white people. That's where the power is. That's where the decisions are made. By the time a black actor walks into a casting director's office, the decision of whether or not a person of color will get that role has been made. Instead of realizing that and either A) making an effort to change the homogenous culture of the industry, or B) leaving it alone and focusing on more pressing issues, the NAACP continues to pound on this subject year after year. It's simple. White people are producing shows starring white people so that white people will watch. Period. I'm not letting them off the hook. I'm just saying that it's not as important as making sure that my vote counts *every* November. Besides, shouldn't we address the horrible programming on the black network before we start pointing fingers at ABC?

We all know that fear of serious head trauma isn't the only reason that blacks are apathetic toward politics and government. The United States of America has failed black people miserably. Let me say that again. This country has failed, and continues to fail black people. From the moment of its inception, America has only paid lip service to the idea that all men are created equal. For some reason, people love to simply gloss over this big fat hairy hypocrisy. Whenever someone points out the sheer lunacy of signing a document that guarantees every man equal treatment under the law while owning another human being as your property, a white guy always springs to the founding father's defense. "Yes, they owned slaves, but those were the times."

Who gives a fuck? Wrong is wrong. Hypocrisy is hypocrisy. Hatred is hatred. Inhumanity is inhumanity. Period. The idea that we should somehow excuse the framers of the constitution for committing the faux pas of owning slaves is disrespectful to the very idea of democracy. Especially if the only defense you can come up with is "everyone else was doing it." I'm assuming at least one of the founding fathers got the classic speech from his mother.

Young John Hancock: "But, Mom, Thomas Jefferson owns slaves."

Mother Hancock: "Don't you give me that young man. If Thomas Jefferson jumped off a cliff, would you do it too?"

Right now, in prisons all across the country, grown men are being forced to perform unspeakable—for straight guys anyway—sexual acts. But that's OK because that's just what goes on in prison right? Guys get raped for a few years, make friends with an older black guy, and then they escape to Mexico. That's not so bad.

The political process has been hostile toward black people

and black people have returned the favor in spades. No pun intended.

"But, Nick. All that stuff happened so long ago. Why would black people be so hostile toward politics and government now?"

Hmmm. Maybe it's because thousands of black voters were disenfranchised in Florida during the 2000 elections? (Don't believe me? Watch the shocking documentary *Unprecedented: The 2000 Presidential Election* or read the enlightening book *Bush Family Fortunes: The Best Democracy Money Can Buy* by Greg Palast.) Maybe it's the fact that there have only been five black United States Senators. Maybe it's the fact that the Republicans sent psychopath and token black guy Alan Keyes to Illinois to try and defeat the fifth of those Senators, Barack Obama. (Vote for *our* black guy. He's better than *theirs*.) Maybe it's the fact that blatant racists like Jesse Helms and Strom Thurmond held their senate positions for a combined seventy-eight years? Maybe it's the fact that during the 2003 Philadelphia mayoral elections, a team of men dressed like federal officials drove around black neighborhoods telling black voters that they needed a major credit card, a passport, or a valid I.D. in order to vote?

Right now my well-intentioned white readers are thinking, "My goodness. No wonder African-Americans don't vote." Fuck you. You don't vote either. Not you, specifically, but a lot of white people. Less than sixty percent of all Americans voted in the 2004 election; which was commonly referred to as the most important election in a generation. And that was the highest voter turnout since 1968. So before you start looking down your nose at the poor, disillusioned black folks, ask yourself this question. What's your excuse? I mean George W. Bush was unfairly appointed to the presidency in 2000 and spent the next four years damaging the environment, lining the pockets of big business, giving tax breaks to the one percent of the population that needed them the least, and sending sons, daughters, mothers, sons, aunts, uncles, brothers, and sisters thousands of miles away to die in a pointless war that he sold to the American people on outdated intelligence, fear-mongering, and downright lies. If that's not enough to get us out to vote, what the hell is? And still mass quantities of educated people who should know better didn't even bother to go to the polls. Shame on us. *All* of us.

Chapter 18

While We're on the Subject . . .

I t's our fault. Don't blame the Republicans. Don't fault the Democrats. The left and the right were both totally secondary. Don't blame Ohio. They weren't the only state that voted for Bush. Blame us. The American people. We are a nation of idiots. Whatever we get during the second Bush term, we brought it on ourselves. We weren't defrauded this time. Our votes were counted, and this is what we chose. By any account, George W. Bush has been one of the worst presidents in history. And our nation decided we wanted four more years of that.

Sure, Bush and his handlers have been great at engineering a marketing campaign that seems to trump the obvious dichotomies. Such as:

Bush would be tougher on terrorism than Kerry would. If Bush hadn't ignored the warning of his terrorism czar, Richard Clarke, the greatest act of terrorism on American soil might have been prevented. Didn't he already drop the ball on the whole terrorism thing? Not to mention the guy that he labeled Public Enemy #1 immediately after 9/11 just conveniently dropped off our radar?

Bush as Average Joe. He comes from old money. Blue

blood money. Legacy at Yale money. Skull & Bones money. Harvard Business School money. He does not like poor people. This means you. During the campaign, I had to listen to so many zombies over country talk about how Bush was going to get their vote because they felt like they could have a beer with him. Have a beer with him?! That just might be the most illogical thinking of all time. Making a decision that is that important by basing it on a single criteria that has absolutely nothing to with that person's ability to do the job. That would be like a woman choosing her gynecologist based solely on that person's best bowling score. Maybe these people actually think they're going to have a beer with the President? When exactly is the White House keg party this year? Nothing beats doing shots of Don Julio with Dick Cheney. It's best not to stay too long though. You'd be surprised how slutty Labor Secretary Elaine Chao gets after she gets a little Peach Schnapps in her. Talk about an awkward morning after.

"So, I see OSHA is taking a tougher stance on workplace fatalities?"

"Yeah, I'm briefing the president in an hour so you gotta get going."

Bush as tough guy. "Bring 'em on." Fuck you, you phony. You had a chance to go and fight, and you didn't. You didn't even have the balls to say, "I don't want to go because I don't believe in this war." You just let your daddy's money save your ass. Bush isn't a tough guy. He's a pussy. He's the worst kind of pussy. He's the guy who's more than willing to fight as long as he's got a few of his drunken frat brothers around to back him up. Get him alone and his conflict resolution skills increase fivefold. He also might curse at you if you're having dinner with your wife and child. Just ask Al Hunt. A drunken

George W. Bush once berated Hunt for something that he didn't even write about then-president George H.W. Bush.

Mission accomplished. Aside from being the biggest publicity stunt since the Madonna/Britney/Christina pseudo-lesbian kiss, it's also factually incorrect. The most intensive fighting of the Iraqi invasion occurred well after our commander in chief played *Top Gun* and declared the mission accomplished. (Thank God he didn't try and play *Top Gun* as a bartender. He would have been throwing those bottles all over the place.) As of this writing, more than 1,000 American soldiers have died since the date that Bush said represented the "end of major combat operations in Iraq." Did all those people trip and fall in the shower? Also, he could have made the landing by helicopter since the USS *Abraham Lincoln* was only 30 miles from San Diego. Navy officers even slowed and turned the ship when land became visible.

The amazing thing is that none of this information is classified. It's all common knowledge if you bother to read a newspaper, a serious magazine, or watch a serious news program which most Americans don't do. Why? Because we are a nation of idiots. We chose instead to focus on so-called moral issues, like gay marriage, that don't affect our own lives in the slightest bit. Unless you're a millionaire, there wasn't one single policy reason why you should have voted for Bush. Education? Worse. Environment? Worse. Economy? Worse. Jobs? Worse. International profile? Worse. In just four years, we went from being wealthy and popular to being in debt and disliked. Can you imagine if you had to endure a change like that during your four years of high school? You'd slit your wrists before even getting to pick out an outfit for the prom. We are a nation of idiots.

People actually allowed the Republicans to turn Kerry's military service against him. John Kerry literally turned his boat around and charged back into the jungle to drag another soldier out, amid heavy gunfire. He's a legitimate war hero. Meanwhile, Bush was on standby in case anyone happened to attack the Dallas-Ft. Worth area.

"Them Gooks is going after the Budweiser plant."

"Not on my watch!"

We are a nation of idiots.

Chapter 19

The Top Black Politicians of All Time

☞ Hiram Revels. At a time when anyone who remembers the 1970s is considered "old school," perhaps we should remember Hiram Rhoades Revels. Even if he weren't on the A-list for being the first black person to serve in the United States Senate, he'd warrant mentioning for rocking the C. Everett Koop beard-with-no-mustache look long before the Surgeon General was even a gleam in his great-great-great-great grandfather's eyes.

☞ Young Al Sharpton. Yes, I said *young* Al Sharpton. He's on the list just for his balls alone. Do you know what kind of stones it takes to be A) a minister and B) a community activist while wearing a track suit, gold medallion, and a perm? That's crazy. Can you imagine a white leader doing anything like that? On second thought, the Attorney General of the United States did sing a cheesy song called "Let the Eagles Soar" at a press conference. That's crazier than the track suit and he still got taken seriously.

☞ Shirley Chisholm. She was the first black woman elected to Congress and the first black person to seek a major party's nomination for the presidency, which already makes her a badass of the highest order. Plus, how many people can say that they got a shout out in a Biz Markie song? Also, her hairdo was "off" the chain. (Were you paying attention earlier, white people?)

☞ J.C. Watts. Former Republican congressman from Oklahoma. The Arnold Drummond of the Republican Party. "Aww, look. It's J.C. Watts the black Republican! Isn't he just adorable?" He was just such an easy target. I'll cut him some slack because I'm pretty sure Oklahoma didn't even free their slaves until the early 1980s. And even then, it was just so that they could play college football.

☞ Barbara Jordan. Congresswoman. Wasn't she great? Stop nodding and go look her up.

☞ Marion Barry. I can't wait for the day, eighteen to twenty-five years from now, when my son or daughter comes to me and says, "So I was reading about this Marion Barry guy. I can't believe that happened!" My memory will probably be fading by then so I'll say something like, "Fred Berry? Yeah he played Rerun on *What's Happening*. He could really dance for a fat guy."

"No dad. Marion Barry. He was mayor of D.C. and got caught smoking crack."

Then, I'll get to enjoy the hilarity of it all over again. Besides, we may have reelected a crackhead as mayor of one city, but white people elected a pro wrestler and a bodybuilder-turned-actor as governors of entire states. And not tiny little states that don't matter like Rhode Island or New Hampshire, big states like Minnesota and California. And for the love of God, if you're going to elect an actor, at least elect a good one. I don't know squat about their politics, but if their acting ability means anything, Martin Sheen and Harrison Ford are at least as capable as Arnold was. I don't think Alec Baldwin has ever played a president, but I'm sure he could just give that "coffee is for closers" speech from *Glengarry Glen Ross* at every campaign stop and people would be lined up at the polls to vote for him. Then, when he's embroiled in some seedy scandal, he could give that "God complex" speech from *Malice* and creep everybody out in a way that Nixon could only dream of.

☞ Joycelyn Elders. Technically, not a politician but, as Surgeon General, she made the following statement: "Masturbation is part of human sexuality and a part of something that perhaps should be taught." She was then fired by President Clinton. Yes. Bill Clinton. The same Bill Clinton who whipped it out for Paula Jones and shoved a cigar in the cooter of Monica Lewinsky. Amazing. Tonight, I'm squeezing some sperm out just for you, Joycelyn.

☞ Charles Rangel. Democratic congressman from New York. Hair like Sharpton, voice like Miles Davis, mustache like Vito Corleone. Leave the tort reform bill. Take the cannoli.

☞ Barack Obama. Democratic Senator from Illinois. Now people can start the black president talk again. And I can

calmly, rationally tell them why they are out of their fucking minds. We're talking about a nation that can't pick the
rightful winner of *American Idol* without the judges inter-
vening. If they didn't want to vote for Fantasia, what
makes you think they're going to vote for Obama?

☞ Alan Keyes. You know the homeless guy who hangs out
across the street from your office building? The one who
randomly screams obscenities at people and you always
laugh, but when you walk by him and you take your deep,
homeless breath—don't feel bad, we all do it—you're kind
of nervous that he might shout at you this time? That's
Alan Keyes. Crazy as a motherfucking bedbug. He's fun
to watch from a distance, but I wouldn't want to get
too close.

Chapter 20

Affirmative Action

T alk about your wedge issues. I don't think you're going to find a lot of people straddling the fence on this one. You either believe it's fair that the government should go out of its way to help minorities, or you think that times have changed enough for people of color to fend for themselves. Before we talk about affirmative action, I should make one thing crystal clear. America owes black people. Yes, still. Sure, times have changed. Yes, things are much, much better for black people now. But the scales are far from balanced. Even if you take this country's policies on absolute face value, segregation was only done away with in the 1960s. That means black people are one generation removed from being prevented access to comparable education, housing, health care, and financial institutions. My mother was in the first class of black people in my town to integrate our local high school. I remember she once found me looking through her old high school yearbook. She spent some time pointing out which one of my classmates had parents who were racist assholes back in the day.

I once tried to explain to a coworker that all these socioeconomic factors have a way of being passed on from one generation to the next. Someone who is educated and financially stable is more likely to have children who are educated and financially stable. It's not a guarantee. It's just more probable. Let's rewind back to great-grandfather Wellman of the Richmond, Virginia, Wellmans. Maybe he finished high school and then worked his way up to manager at the tobacco processing plant. He made good money, invested wisely, and insisted that all his children attend college. After school, his son returns home to take an executive position at Philip Morris, working his way up to Senior Vice President. His children don't even think about not going to college and both give in to his pressure and get graduate degrees as well. By the time their kids come along they have all the benefits of growing up around nothing but educated and successful people.

My great grandfather signed his name with an X. I watched him do it. Do you see what I'm getting at?

Am I oversimplifying? Yes. There are tons of white people who grew up in poor, uneducated families. There are a lot of black people who had affluent upbringings. The difference is . . . it was never illegal for white people to learn how to read. There weren't elaborate, totally legal schemes put in place to stop white men from voting. Little white children never had to be escorted to class by National Guardsmen. White people were never allowed to suffer from syphilis, not told that they had the disease, and become of interest to the United States Public Heath Service only when it was time for their autopsy.

For several generations, the United States government waged a public, multifaceted, heinous, ingenious, and incredibly successful war on black people. As a result, we tend to be less educated, less healthy, and less financially secure. Either you believe that, or you believe that blacks are simply inferior human beings.

Not to mention that black people aren't the only ones benefiting from affirmative action. White women are too. But you don't hear about that much do you? People in this country are quick to complain about welfare mothers in the inner city, but no one ever mentions the millions of dollars in corporate welfare that gets handed out every year. People are quick to point the finger when the big, black running back gets a full scholarship to the University of Michigan just because he's good at football, but no one ever mentions the short, pasty blonde who gets into a university because her last name is Vanderbilt or Rockefeller or Paltrow. Yes, that Paltrow. Seems like Gwyneth was such a dummy that she couldn't get in anywhere and family friend Steven Spielberg had to pull some strings to get her into UC Santa Barbara.

We have to stop thinking of affirmative action as a handout or reverse racism, and start seeing it for what it really is: An attempt by the United States government to right a wrong. It's either affirmative action or reparations and I'm guessing there aren't enough acres or enough mules to pull that one off.

Chapter 21

God? Damn It.

There is a long, rich tradition of Christianity in the black community. The only time that slaves were allowed to congregate in large groups was to worship. The church was the heart and soul of the civil rights movement, serving as meeting place, news dispenser, etc. I was brought up in a big Southern Baptist church. I remember sitting on those hard pews, wearing my Sunday best, taking in the entire spectacle with wide-eyed awe. Going to church was like going to the circus every Sunday. Except it smelled a lot better. And there were no clowns. (Who in the hell came up with the idea of using clowns to entertain children? I don't know one single human being who doesn't find clowns creepy.) There was some horrendous makeup and some really bad suits at church, but there were no actual clowns. The singing, the praying, the sermon, people getting so full of emotion that they had to be restrained. All of that can have a powerful effect on a young person.

In the face of that, I was struck with the notion that after all the things we've gone through as a people, we still believe. We still have faith in God. I started to think about the Middle Passage. I started to think about slavery, about Jim Crow, about the Civil Rights movement. After pondering all those things, it became clear to me.

God does not like black people. Or Indians or Jews for that matter. Let the truth be told. God is a racist fuck. Since the beginning of recorded history, in every corner of the globe, white people have killed and oppressed people of various shades of red, yellow, and brown in the name of God. And what did this asshole do to stop it? Nothing. He allowed the Germans to march the Jews into ovens. He allowed 90% of the Native Americans on this continent to be destroyed. He allowed black people to be legally counted as 3/5ths of a man. He allowed the United States government to round up and incarcerate Japanese-Americans during World War II. He allowed European nations to carve up sub-Saharan Africa to the extent that many of those governments are still in a shambles. He allowed the Australians to shit on the Aborigines. He allowed the New Zealanders to shit on the Maori.

Don't try to cover for him either. He has no excuse. He's omnipotent and omniscient. He knew this was going on and he had the power to stop it, so blatant dislike of minorities is the only real excuse he has. Considering that his only son was a Jew, I'd say that the man upstairs has some serious self-hatred issues.

Can you imagine getting all the way up to the pearly gates, only to have St. Peter tell you, "We don't welcome your kind here, nigger. Go to hell." Literally. Maybe they let a few blacks into heaven. Sammy Davis Jr. gets in, but he has to use the service entrance and eat in the kitchen. Screw it. I'd rather be in hell anyway. That's where all the fun will be. Plus, I lived in Tucson for two years so I'd be totally acclimated to the weather. Except hell will probably be much more humid than Tucson.

Making Friends With Black People

Tucson is a dry heat. (Since there are no black people there, it's also a white heat. So, it might get hot in Tucson, but no one is going to start a riot. It doesn't get *Do the Right Thing* hot.) Hell could be a blast. You can keep your harp music and robes. I'd rather golf with O.J. and hang out all night partying with Jack Johnson, Old Dirty Bastard, and my great-grandfather. Besides, people always focus on the good aspects of heaven. What about the downside. No matter where you go, if there is a collection of human beings—or deceased human beings—there is bound to be a pecking order. It's human nature to find a way to rank each other in some sort of hierarchy. In heaven, the only thing that everyone would have in common would be that they're all dead. So, that would probably become the measuring stick. All of the cool people in heaven will be the ones who died in some sort of heroic or tragic way.

"So, how did you die anyway?"

"I was on my way to volunteer at the local soup kitchen when I saw this orphanage on fire. I ran in and helped evacuate all the children, but I died from smoke inhalation."

"Wow. That's amazing."

"Well, you would have done the same thing. So what happened to you?"

"You know the warning on the mayonnaise jar that says 'refrigerate after opening'?"

"Sure."

"That is not a suggestion. That's a requirement. I found out the hard way."

But that's just one of the many reasons why I've never been religious. Here's another. If your religion is so great, why do you have to sell it so hard? I was picking someone up from LAX one night when this Hare Krishna approached me. I thought to my-

171

self, "Dude. If you're standing in the airport at 9:30 on a Thursday night trying to get people to join your religion . . . it can't be that great." During the hay days of the Lakers, you never saw men in funny outfits standing outside of Staples Center yelling, "Have you taken Kobe Bean Bryant as your savior? Do you have a few minutes to hear about the gospel of Shaquille?"

Why would you want everyone to take to your religion anyway? If everyone got on board, then everyone would be going to heaven right? What is the easiest way to ruin a great bar or nightclub? Exactly. Let in all kinds of over-the-hill swinging singles, recently turned twenty-one frat boys and sorority girls, and hipsters who read about the place in the Style section of the newspaper on Friday morning. Most places worth hanging out in must maintain some air of exclusivity. I can say all of this because I don't believe in any of it. I don't call myself an atheist because I don't believe that strongly that there isn't a God. I guess you could call me an agnostic because I've come to believe that the only intelligent conclusion that I can draw is that I don't know what higher power may or may not exist. I can say that without worry now. Not because I've just come to grips with where my soul might end up. I did that a long time ago. I can say that because there was only one person who existed that I wouldn't want to think any less or differently of me. And she's dead. Once my mother died as a result of Lupus, it really solidified and confirmed my non-religious beliefs. I should elaborate.

There are various religions and they all have various rules to follow. Abide by the rules and you go to heaven. Break those rules and you go to whatever that particular group believes in as hell. The rules are so specific that someone has to be right, which means that everyone else is wrong. For the sake of argument, let's say that the Muslims had it right. My mother was a fundamentally good person. She worked, raised her children, and went to church. She lived a good Christian life. But, according to Islam, she's burning in hell right now because she ate pork and showed her calves in public. No disrespect to the approximately 1 billion Muslims throughout the world, but that's just plain silly.

Chapter 22

Help Nick Choose a Religion

O K. So the southern Baptist thing clearly didn't take. But it wouldn't be fair to give up on all organized religion based on my experiences with one sect would it? I think I have to give it another shot. Let's examine the pros and cons of some other potential religions.

Judaism

Pro: Bar Mitzvah baby! What? Thirteen-years-old, my ass. If I'm converting, I'm having a Bar Mitzvah, you meshugine.[1]

Con: I'm not giving up pork for anyone. Not even Jehovah himself.

Pro: Even more historical oppression than mine for hilarious comedy material.

Con: Is thirty-two too old for a Bris?

[1] *Yiddish for "crazy person."*

Catholicism

Pro: Wine at church? Very classy.

Con: The whole "not turning pedophiles in to the authorities" thing would make me feel real icky.

Pro: All of the sitting, standing, and kneeling at church gives Catholics amazing quads and glutes.

Con: The penance for masturbating to *Getting Fit with Denise Austin* when I was thirteen . . . 476 rosaries.

Rastafarianism

Pro: Not only is marijuana use accepted . . . it's basically a requirement.

Con: I'm pretty much locked in to the bald look from here on out. Are pubic dreadlocks OK?

Pro: Wait. What were we talking about? Pass the chips.

Con: Me woman not be able to understand what em saying, seen?[2]

Buddhism

Pro: Kick ass Buddhist monk kung fu skills.

Con: Beastie Boys Free Tibet concerts. I will *not* be preached to by Mike D. These are the same guys who recorded *Brass Monkey*.

Pro: Blissful, enlightened state.

Con: I can get a blissful, enlightened state by being a Rastafarian. And I don't have to wear those sissy orange robes.

[2] *My wife wouldn't be able to understand what I was saying. Understand?*

176

Jehovah's Witness

Pro: Walking from door to door is an excellent, low-impact, aerobic workout.

Con: At least the Jews understood that if you take Christmas away, you're got to replace it with something.

Pro: Apparently we are now near the "time of the end." At least I wouldn't have to deal with this painfully dull religion for that long.

Con: Only 144,000 will make it into heaven. The other 6.4 million practicing Jehovah's Witnesses are going to be shit outta luck.

Scientology

Pro: Tom Cruise, John Travolta, and Isaac Hayes go to my church. Who goes to yours?

Con: Those motherfuckers are crazy! Did you see *Battlefield Earth*? Second worst movie ever. (The title of worst movie ever will be held in perpetuity by *Night of the Lepus*; a sci-fi flick about giant, mutant, killer . . . wait for it . . . bunny rabbits. OK. I can't not talk more about *Battlefield Earth*. True story. I'm watching HBO one Sunday afternoon and I see that the movie is coming on. I figured I should see what all the fuss was about. During the opening credits I actually say out loud, "This is horrible." The movie was *that* bad. Acting, writing, plot, wardrobe, hair, makeup. Believe it or not, that film contained some of the worst best boy grip work I've ever seen on a film. Bertrand Dupuis, you should be ashamed of yourself. But back to Scientology.)

Pro: Screw CAA and William Morris. This is the most powerful agency in Hollywood.

Con: How can we make our new organized religion sound even less appealing? I got it. Let's put the word science in the name!

Mormonism

Pro: Multiple wives.

Con: Multiple wives.

Pro: Being *the* black Mormon would afford me semi-celebrity status.

Con: Mind numbingly dull "hub" cities Salt Lake City, Utah, and Boise, Idaho. (Random hilarious sports quote. Years ago, NBA veteran Derrick Harper was going to be traded from the then-lowly Dallas Mavericks to a John Stockton and Karl Malone–led title contender in Utah. He exercised a clause in his contract that allowed him to veto the trade. When asked why, he replied, "You go live in Utah. I don't want to live in Utah.")

Santeria

Pro: Freaky rituals with hot-blooded island women increase odds of amazing sexual experiences.

Con: Freaky rituals with hot-blooded island women increase odds of "machete incident." FYI, there is no such thing as a good "machete incident."

Pro: Easy access to fresh chicken and goat meat for grilling.

Con: It is impossible to get chicken blood out of suede.

Native American Shamanism

Pro: Peyote.

Con: Tedious conversations with well-meaning, liberal white people about how fascinating your religion is.

Pro: Lax dress code. Shirtless with buckskin pants beats suit and tie every day of the week.

Con: Burning sage irritates my eyes.

Hindu

Pro: Vishnu. Coolest God ever. Possibility that I could play for the Lakers or be a rock star in a future incarnation.

Con: No beef, no Nick.

Pro: Easy opening line for picking up hippie chicks.

Con: I would probably have to be offended by Apu from *The Simpsons*.

Satanism

Pro: All my bad habits are no longer bad habits.

Con: Spending time with Goths.

Pro: I already have a long and detailed list of people that I would love to sacrifice. Bill O'Reilly, lock your doors.

Con: Listening to albums backwards.

Chapter 23

Slam Dunk

This is for everyone who is wringing their hands over young black males going directly from high school to the NBA.

MAN SLAIN, TWO WOUNDED AT HOOP STAR'S BUILDING
By Philip Messing, Larry Celona and Erin Calabrese

February 9, 2004—Three men were shot last night, one fatally, on the third floor of a Brooklyn housing project near the apartment of high-school basketball star Sebastian Telfair, police said. The shootings took place at the Surfside Garden Houses on West 31st Street in Coney Island at about 7:15 P.M.

One of the victims was pronounced dead at the scene. He died inside an elevator.

The two other victims were found in the hallway. One was taken to Lutheran Hospital, the other to Coney Island Hospital, both in critical condition.

Police gave no motive for the shootings, but sources said one of the victims was arrested for another shooting in the building last year.

Jo Li Wingata, 48, who said she was a cousin of the dead man, said she believed it was drug-related.

Telfair is a star point guard at Lincoln HS who will be a top pick in this year's NBA draft should he pass up college at Louisville, where he said he'd go.

He lives on the floor where the shooting took place, sources said.

Telfair was not home at the time. Police did not believe any of the victims were related to him. Knicks point guard Stephon Marbury, who also starred at Lincoln and grew up in the project, is Telfair's cousin.

Police were leaning toward the theory that the shooter was one of the three victims, but hadn't completely ruled out the possibility that there was a fourth person involved.

"It's happened one too many times out here," Wingata said. "All these kids they want to fight one another.

"They're thinking fast money. It's all about drugs—all about drugs." The project has recovered from some rocky times recently. Major crimes rose 47 percent from 2001 to 2002, but then dropped back to the 2001 level last year.

NYPD Daily Blotter 2/09/04

Now, put yourself in his place. You're a high school basketball sensation. You're eighteen years old and you're already appeared on the cover of *Sports Illustrated* and played games on national television. You've been playing elite-level basketball year-round for years. Adidas wants to sign you to a multimillion dollar contract. The word on the NBA grapevine is that you'll probably be taken in the first round of the NBA draft which means your contract is guaranteed. Oh yeah. Also, Rick Pitino wants you to come to come and play for him at Louisville. You can go enjoy four years of being treated like a king in the rolling hills of Kentucky while your mother, stepfather, and younger brother continue to negotiate the dangerous hallways of the housing projects, or you can sign your name on two pieces of paper and take care of them for life. What would you do? Exactly. Now shut the fuck up and go worry about all of those gymnasts and figure skaters who are busting their asses and starving themselves—for no money I might add—for one shot at Olympic gold; only to be completely erased from this country's collective memory four years later when the next young sensation comes along.

Chapter 24

How to Fit in on a Basketball Court

People often talk about sports as a way of uniting the population. Just as often, it ends up driving a wedge between us. Pick-up basketball is a huge part of the maturation process of the black male. There are various and sundry unwritten rules that exist on the court that white people must master if they're going to take part in this ritual of manhood. They are as follows:

☞ Black men do not buy $150 shoes to play basketball in. We buy them to look good at the mall and at parties. We buy our basketball shoes on sale, or at Ross or TJ Maxx.

☞ Socks are worn either very high or very low. Anything mid-calf is a sure sign of either an amateur or an old man.

☞ Black people don't "shoot hoops" or "shoot some baskets." We "shoot hoop" (singular), we "shoot ball," we "hoop," we "ball," or we "run."

☞ The headband look is a tough one to pull off. I'd suggest avoiding it.

☞ When your feet hit the court, your hat comes off. Period.

☞ Don't argue every little call. That's for kids and the guys who are superstars in their own minds. If you really think you're getting screwed, just make a mental note to make up for it. Later on in the game, if you miss a shot or lose the ball out of bounds, call a foul whether you were fouled or not. Do it with conviction and don't entertain any arguments. Enjoy your free pass.

☞ Showing up to the court in a brand-new, matching And 1 ensemble is like wearing a shirt that says "I have no basketball skills at all. Do not pick me." In basketball, overcompensation is a big no-no.

☞ Please do not wear your tiny little white guy running shorts to play basketball. No one at the courts wants to see pasty white guy upper thigh and fringe pubic hair.

☞ Only assholes or good friends trash talk.

☞ Do not take any charges. You'll probably get a concussion because you haven't done it since your sophomore year in college, and you'd definitely get laughed off the court.

☞ If you can't shoot or dribble, don't shoot too much and don't dribble too much. Just play good defense, rebound, and set some screens. *Everybody* loves to play with that guy. Also, when you hit your thirties and your knees give out on you, you're going to become that guy anyway. Why not give yourself a head start?

☞ No substitutions unless there is an injury. If your buddy doesn't get picked, he gets to sit his ass down and wait for the next game. And if you're so tired that you can't last the entire game, you need to drag your pathetic old carcass home, take a bath, pour yourself a mug of chamomile, and read a good book. Pussy.

☞ I love watching *Streetball* as much as the next guy, but if you hit me in the head with the basketball . . . I'm kicking your ass. Professor.

☞ Pull your shorts up. Why do white people always have to take *everything* too far?

☞ If you win, you stay. Period. Don't you dare fuck up our team chemistry because your wife wants to get to Bed, Bath & Beyond before 2 P.M.

☞ Unless you are at Venice Beach, there aren't any pretty girls watching. Just leave your shirt on you sweaty, hairy beast.

Chapter 25

NASCAR

White people, before you get too full of yourself deriding black Americans' obsession with loud, bass-heavy music and flashy jewelry, remind yourself of one thing. NASCAR. We may be willing to pay money to see 50 Cent mumble incoherently for a few hours, but you guys pay to sit out in the hot sun and watch cars driven around in a circle for four hours.

Before I go any further, I should clarify my position on NASCAR. It's more boring than watching grass grow, and I can't imagine why any human being would spend more than 5 seconds watching it. I don't even know what you could do to the sport that would make the sport even remotely interesting to me. Maybe if *High Times* magazine sponsored a car. While everyone else is careering around the track at speeds of 180 mph, the *High Times* mobile is hugging the far right wall and creeping along at a slow, but steady 35. Every fifth lap the car would put on its left turn blinker and ease over into pit row for sodas and snacks.

The most amazing thing about NASCAR—besides the fact that people actually pay to watch it—is the fact that the drivers and their crew chiefs actually discuss strategy before a race? How much fucking strategy does it take to drive really fast in circles?

"Listen, Earl. Here's the plan. What I'm gonna do is drive really fast down this straightaway, then turn left, then do the same thing on the other side of the track. If I can keep that up . . . I've got a pretty good shot at winning this damn thing. "

NASCAR fans will lecture you on the amount of skill that it takes to drive a state-of-the-art vehicle at those speeds. First of all, the cars on the NASCAR circuit are all Fords, Dodges, and Chevys. I'm going to be only so impressed with someone driving a Ford, no matter how souped-up it is. I'd rather watch a plastic surgeon in the midst of a midlife crisis drive his brand-new Porsche Carrera through rush hour traffic on the 405 freeway in Los Angeles than watch a fucking Dodge zooming around an oval. And sure, it does take a lot of skill to do what NASCAR drivers do, but so does performing a root canal and I don't want to watch that on TV either. And a root canal is much, much shorter than a NASCAR race.

Chapter 26

Indians

There are two groups of people that black folks just don't get to complain to. Holocaust survivors and Native Americans. A black person complaining to an Indian is like a paraplegic complaining to a quadriplegic. No one even thinks about Indians because most people have forgotten that they even exist. When I told my mom that I was dating an Indian girl, her reply was, "We still have those?" This was, of course, after she asked the mandatory "Indian from India?"

We hear the word "genocide" thrown around so often on the news these days that you don't even think about it. As horrible as the events in Sudan, Iraq, etc. have been, in none of those situations has an entire race of people been wiped out. Not even close. America gave it the old college try. As a result, there aren't a lot of Indians around. If you can't make enough noise, no one is ever going to hear you. Rest assured, the only reason there's no pro sports team named the Coons is that black folks would raise all holy hell.

The only reason that I even think about these issues is that I'm married to an Indian person. The only reason that I even know that there are Indians around is because I spend the holidays with them. To answer your question, yes. Indians do cele-brate Thanksgiving. Although the tone is more like thanks . . . thanks a lot giving. Currently, in Indian country, there is a movement to ensure that young kids can speak their tribal lan-guage. In some tribes, there is a very real danger of the native tongue dying out. When was the last time an entire fucking lan-guage died out? Can you imagine if no one in all of Chinatown could read the signs?

The first time I met the man who would one day become my father-in-law, I was nervous as hell. In college, I had developed a habit of referring to people by a group of randomly assigned nick-names like Chief, Smooth, Money, Main Man, etc. That way, if I had forgotten—or never bothered to learn—someone's name, I had an easy out. Moreover, people would leave the exchange feeling that we were closer than we really were because I had given them a nickname. Some might say that this is a dickhead, hipster kind of thing to do. To anyone who says that, I say, "Fuck you . . . whatever your name is." Anyway, I was terrified that I would be introduced to her dad and respond in a rambling re-sponse similar to John Cusak as Lloyd Dobler in *Say Anything*.

"Nice to meet you, chief. Oh. I didn't mean like an actual chief. I mean . . . unless you are an actual chief. In that case . . . what's up? But you wouldn't say 'what's up' to a chief would you? Isn't there some sort of official greeting? Would I have to bow or something? But, if you were a chief you would have like a headdress or something, right? I guess you couldn't just wear that around all day. Do they make like a smaller, informal head-dress? One to wear like on casual Friday? You know, if you're just chilling around the sweat lodge."

Don't worry. That didn't happen. I just shook his hand and introduced myself. And for the record, he isn't a chief.

Conclusion

So what have we learned? We've learned that an unknown stand-up comedian had a lot of time on his hands while he was living in Tucson, Arizona. We've learned that the Icelandic people are fucking disgusting. Most importantly we've learned that you apparently had $14 to waste. (Seriously, you bought this instead a paperback copy of *A Tale of Two Cities*? What were you thinking?)

Hopefully, you've found this book to be humorous. If so, then my primary mission has been accomplished. If you found yourself thinking about any of the aforementioned issues or ideas for the first time or even in a new light, then that's gravy. Americans are a long way from taking part in an open, honest dialogue on race. Maybe if we can laugh and joke about it—with no malice in our hearts—we'll at least make some progress.